fine art
wire weaving

weaving techniques
for stunning jewelry designs

sarah thompson

INTERWEAVE.
interweave.com

Interweave
A division of F+W Media, Inc.
4868 Innovation Drive
Fort Collins, CO 80525
interweave.com

Manufactured in USA by RR Donnelley Roanoke

Library of Congress Cataloging-in-Publication Data

Thompson, Sarah, 1981-
  Fine art wire weaving : weaving techniques for stunning jewelry designs
/ Sarah Thompson.
     pages cm
  Includes index.
  ISBN 978-1-63250-025-0
1. Jewelry making. 2. Wire jewelry. 3. Weaving. I. Title.
  TT212.T5626 2015
  745.594'2--dc23
                       2014049509

EDITOR	Michelle Mach
TECHNICAL EDITORS	Jane Dickerson and Bonnie Brooks
PHOTOGRAPHERS	Matt Graves and Ann Sabin Swanson
ART DIRECTOR	Charlene Tiedemann
DESIGNER	Karla Baker

acknowledgments

There are so many people to say thank you to for helping me get to this point. Without them I would not have been here to write this book. I need to first say thank you to my parents: to my mom, who helped foster the creative spirit and encouraged me to never stop exploring and learning, and to my dad, who has always been there to help out with any project and who first presented this book idea to me and had faith before I ever did that I could become an author and a teacher.

I have been blessed to teach in wonderful stores. Thank you, Beads and Beyond, for taking a chance on a brand-new teacher who had no clue whether she could teach yet; you gave me a wonderful teaching experience and the confidence to continue teaching. Thank you, Fusion Beads, for the continual support and patience with me as I grew as a teacher. You challenged me in many ways to be a better teacher.

Thank you to all my students, who have been enthusiastically supportive and gave me wonderful insight into what I wanted to put in the book.

And last but definitely not the least, I would like to thank my husband, Brian, who has been amazingly supportive in all that I do and has encouraged me from day one. Thank you for taking the time to go through my projects and help me write them better, thank you for listening to all my ideas, and thank you for stepping in and taking care of the kids. And thank you to my kids, who stepped up and cleaned the house and cooked dinners while I was writing. Without their support, the book would never have been finished.

contents

the projects

introduction

My journey in jewelry making began when I received my first stash of beads at age fourteen. I quickly became fixated with learning all I could with this medium and spent many hours haunting the library and local bead store for new books and magazines. As my skills grew, I began to gravitate toward off-loom beadwork. While I loved the diversity and dimensions I could achieve by building layers of beadwork, I wanted to continue to grow and learn other forms of jewelry making as well.

My desire to make more elegant, flowing designs that were both delicate and wearable led to my experiments with wire. I found most traditional wirework too simple. The more complex wirework jewelry that I could find looked free-form, organic, rustic, and bulky, not the precise and refined look I wanted. I also struggled with the wire; it felt awkward and unnatural, which led to frustration.

My breakthrough came in 2005, when I was introduced to Marilyn Moore's work for the first time. I instantly fell in love with her beautiful vases made from recycled copper wire. I admired the movement, textures, and sculptural qualities in the woven wire. This was what I was looking for; I saw how I could use these techniques to make the jewelry I had always envisioned.

Over the next five years, I experimented, trying to turn my vision into a reality. My success came when I began melding the same concepts I learned from years of beadwork into wirework. The weave became the peyote stitch. Once I realized this, I found I could manipulate the wire the same way I would if I were beading. I experimented with different wire types and sizes. I pulled ideas from crochet to better handle the wire. I layered the wire together one step at a time to add depth and details.

Many wireworkers use 26-gauge wire as their smallest size; I found that 28- to 30-gauge wire makes weaving more delicate and finely textured. By combining the weaves with shaping, layering, symmetry, and three-dimensional forming, wirework bursts with a whole new level of possibilities.

In 2010, I started teaching. I enjoy giving students a strong foundation for creating their own original designs. The beginning projects in this book focus on the weave to help you practice and become proficient and consistent in your workmanship. As you progress through the book, you'll learn more advanced design elements and create more complex projects. By the time you finish, I hope you'll feel confident about combining different elements. Have fun experimenting and finding your own unique style.

sarah

materials

choosing the right wire for the job

Wire comes in a wide range of sizes, shapes, hardnesses, and metals. You can create beautiful work with all types of wire, but working with the right wire will cut down on frustration and result in a more beautifully finished piece.

When it comes to wire, I like to keep it simple. Instead of having round, half-round, and square wire on hand, I choose to work only with round wire. Round wire is very versatile. If I want a flat surface, I hammer it. If I need a section to be a half-round, I file it. I sort my wire gauges into three categories: heavy, medium, and small. Use heavy (14- to 20-gauge) wire

to provide structure for bases; it can be shaped, woven, and layered together to create a complex design. Use medium (22- to 26-gauge) wire to add beads into the finished forms, create head pins and links, and wrap briolettes—essentially, everything pertaining to embellishments. Use small (28-gauge and smaller) wire to weave and sew the base wires together, adding stability, strength, cohesiveness, and texture to the design.

Because many designs require extreme shaping, the wire must have certain qualities. First, how soft is it? I want the softest, most malleable wire possible. Just because a wire is labeled "dead-soft" doesn't mean it's as soft as I would like. There's a difference in wire malleability among manufacturers. Second, how quickly does it harden and get brittle? This is particularly important with the smaller gauges because the more you work with wire, the harder it gets. This is called work-hardened. You want to weave without having the wire break every time it gets a kink and to shape heavy-gauge wires with ease. Other qualities include whether the wire can be annealed (heated with a flame so it becomes soft and malleable), hammered, or oxidized, and how nicely the end balls up when torched.

FINE SILVER

Also known as pure silver or .999 silver, this is my wire of choice. It's the most malleable, easily shaped into intricate designs. It can be reshaped if needed and anneals wonderfully. Fine silver does not get as brittle as sterling silver does, so the 28-gauge wire won't break as frequently when used. The finished weave also compacts better with less spring to it. Fine silver melts easily, creating smooth balls on the tips of the wire. The best part is that the wire doesn't need to be pickled after torching. Having young children at home, I prefer to avoid caustic chemicals. This wire is also slow to oxidize, so it won't require frequent polishing.

STERLING SILVER

I rarely use sterling silver. Once you start working with this wire, it quickly starts to harden, making it difficult to finish intricate, three-dimensional shaping. It also means more breakage while weaving. It's difficult to reshape after a mistake. It doesn't torch as easily as fine silver does; the balls on the end of the wire tend to be slightly pitted. After torching, you'll have to pickle the wire to remove the firescale. Sterling silver can be annealed, but this will darken the wire and can be cumbersome to do when the wires are woven together. You can weave with 28-gauge wire, but the weave tends to spring up and doesn't compact nicely. I use it for base wires when I want a structurally sound base such as a bracelet. I also try to keep my design simpler when using sterling silver. Also, the copper content in sterling silver means it oxidizes much more quickly than fine silver does.

ARGENTIUM SILVER

This newer form of sterling silver does not oxidize as quickly as traditional sterling silver. Although it is possible to anneal this wire, it needs to be heated and cooled just right or it becomes very brittle. It also becomes brittle to the point that it will break if

heated too long or hammered. It doesn't form nice round balls when heated, but curls onto itself. Even the dead-soft wire hardens quickly, making it difficult to shape into complex designs. All of these qualities make this wire difficult to work with.

COPPER

I prefer working with dead-soft copper wire rather than sterling silver. However, not all dead-soft copper is equal. Make sure it is raw and uncoated without any antitarnish coating, or it will not oxidize. I buy my copper in ¼- to 1-pound (114 to 454g) spools. I have found most copper wire sold in smaller packages tends to be harder and more difficult to use. If you're struggling with your copper wire, try a different source. You can torch copper and create balls on the tips of the wire, but the balls are pitted. You also have to pickle the wire after torching to remove the firescale. Copper can be annealed just like fine silver and sterling silver, and it oxidizes really quickly.

To keep my silver wire organized, I use a torch to ball up the tip on one end on my fine silver wire so I can distinguish it from my sterling silver wire at a glance. This way I can store all my silver wire together, yet easily tell it apart.

CRAFT WIRE

Craft wire tends to break frequently. I would use this wire for weaving only if I wanted to add a vibrant color in the weaving sections added to my design. If this is your only option for copper wire, be sure to choose "bare copper" if you want to oxidize your pieces. "Natural copper" has an antitarnish coating, which prevents it from oxidizing.

PLATED OR FILLED WIRE

This wire limits your design possibilities. It cannot be hammered, and the ends cannot be melted. The plating can rub off when polishing, revealing the copper core. I make an exception for gold-filled wire because of the price of gold.

beads

The projects in this book mainly use crystals and pearls, which are easy to find and come in standard sizes and shapes. Feel free to switch out the beads to fit your own personal tastes.

Some things to consider when selecting beads for jewelry making:

- *Can you fit the desired wire gauge through the bead hole?*

- *How many times will you need to string the wire through the bead?*

- *Can you change the wire gauge to accommodate the bead?*

- *Do you plan to tumble the piece? Is the bead durable enough to go through the tumbler?*

- *If not, can you easily add the bead with some pre-oxidized wire after tumbling the piece?*

When shopping for wire, note that there is a tolerance in the manufacturing of the wire. Wire labeled 30-gauge can actually be a 29-gauge wire. Because it falls within the tolerance, it is considered acceptable.

a note about pearls

Because pearls are porous, it is always a good idea to place a spare pearl in the liver of sulfur solution to see how it reacts. The dyes used to color the pearls can bleed out or change. The same can be said for other porous or dyed stones. Alternatively, you can choose to add these beads after the project is oxidized and polished with some pre-oxidized wire. If you do oxidize your project with the pearl in place, be mindful of the pearl as you polish and avoid scratching the pearl with your steel wool.

tools

I started with a $15 set of pliers. Although they got the job done, I developed a mild hand pain that lasted all day. When I switched to ergonomic pliers, the pain left, and my work vastly improved. You don't need top-of-the-line tools, but it's worth it to invest in the best tools you can. A good set of pliers, cutters, a chasing hammer, and a bench block are staples. And don't forget that your hands are the best tools; use them to shape the wire as much as possible.

wire-forming tools

PLIERS (FLAT-NOSE, ROUND-NOSE, CHAIN-NOSE)

Use these for most wire bending and shaping. If you can, invest in an ergonomic pair to cut down on hand fatigue. When choosing flat-nose pliers, I recommend smooth pliers with a smaller, thinner nose to make crisper angles. Round-nose pliers should taper to a small diameter; the smaller the diameter, the tighter the loops you can form.

WIRE OR FLUSH CUTTERS

I prefer cutting with flush cutters that can cut up to 14-gauge wire. They save time because I don't need to file the ends flush. They're especially handy for making organic loops. Choose a pair with pointed tips for better access to tight areas, allowing you to trim the wire as flush as possible.

CHASING HAMMER

Look for a hammer with some weight, but not so heavy that it's uncomfortable. The head should be smooth and without dents. Using a hammer with rounded edges helps prevent tool marks, especially for beginners. I personally like Fretz hammers because they are weighted, so you can use less force when hammering.

STEEL BENCH BLOCK

You want a smooth, undented steel bench block that is between 3 and 4 inches (7.5 and 10 cm) wide. You can place a rubber insert, sandbag, or even a folded washcloth under it to muffle the sound.

RAWHIDE MALLET

I prefer a rawhide mallet, but a rubber or silicone mallet works well, too. Use the mallet to shape or form the wire or woven strips around a mandrel without marring the work.

RING MANDREL

I like steel tapered metal ring-sizing mandrels instead of the stepped variety. I use mine any time I want a curved design, not just a ring.

BRACELET MANDREL

A round or an oval bracelet mandrel comes in handy when forming bracelets. My favorite is the step-down bracelet mandrel. When making bracelets with clasps, I use the mandrel to achieve a nice curvature, rather than size the bracelet. Bracelet mandrels can be an expensive tool and may not be practical for everyone. An alternative method is to shape the bracelet by hand or around a large pipe, the dowel in your coat closet, small soup cans, or a canning jar. Get creative with what you have around the house.

DOWELS

Having a variety of dowels in different sizes will help you create consistently shaped curves and loops. Anything round will work, including knitting needles or crochet hooks. While not specifically used in the projects, bail-making pliers are particularly handy because they contain several dowel sizes in one tool. You can also mark your round-nose pliers and use the mark as a guide to create same-sized loops.

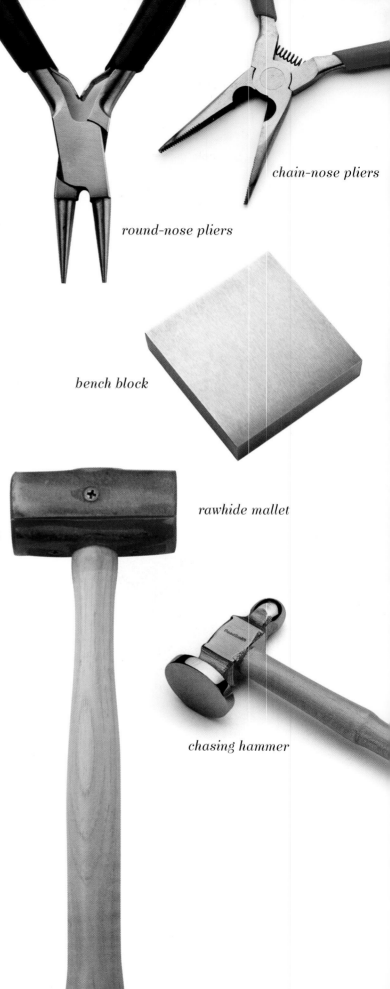

chain-nose pliers

round-nose pliers

bench block

rawhide mallet

chasing hammer

general tools

RING CLAMP

Use a ring clamp to hold the base wires as you weave. Not only is it ergonomic and comfortable to hold, but also the leather in the clamp tightly grips the wire without marring it.

BEADING AWL

This must-have tool punctures the weave so you can "sew" beads or wire to the weave. It also comes in handy to fish out the 28-gauge wire from a tight spot. Choose a beading awl with a tapered, sharp point. If you don't have one, a "T" pin also works well.

HANDHELD METAL HOLE PUNCH

Use this to punch holes into paddled wires. You'll need the 1.25 mm and 1.8 mm hole punch sizes.

FILES

Needle files provide more control in small spaces than larger hand files do. I use flat and oval files most often. You can use the larger hand files to file wire ends flat.

BOBBINS

I use 1½-inch (3.8 cm) bobbins to prevent wire from kinking and tangling while working. The fewer kinks in your wire, the less often it will break. It will also lessen the time spent detangling wire.

PAINTER'S TAPE

Use this low-stick blue tape to hold the base wires together as you begin to weave. It leaves little or no residue when removed.

FABRIC TAPE

You can find this pliable tape in the bandage section of a supermarket. The 1-inch (2.5 cm)-wide strips protect your fingers from wire rubbing against them.

painter's tape

RULER

Choose a ruler with markings down to at least ⅛ inch (3 mm). I like using a 12-inch (30.5 cm) metal ruler because it's easy to remove permanent marker from the metal. A ruler with centimeters comes in handy to measure the diameter of dowels.

FINE-POINT PERMANENT MARKER

Not all permanent markers are the same; a good one should not rub off easily. I use a Bic permanent marker.

WIRE GAUGE

Use this to measure the diameter or gauge of the wire.

MAGNIFICATION

It can be difficult to see fine-gauge wires. When choosing a magnification tool, keep in mind that you can be weaving for hours. A tool that requires you to lean over will cause back strain over time. My students most often use reading glasses or OptiVISORs. Another favorite is Euro Tool's lightweight neck magnifier that hangs around your neck and allows you to watch TV while you work.

LIGHTING

Good lighting helps prevent eye fatigue and allows you to see the fine-textured weave better.

WORK SURFACE

You'll want a flat, solid surface for hammering. When I'm weaving a large section, I'll move to the couch for comfort, then go back to my work station to finish the rest of the jewelry.

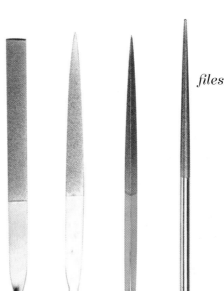

files

torch tools

BUTANE MICRO TORCH

Micro torches come in different temperatures. The lower the flame temperature, the longer it takes to ball up the wire. This micro torch is great for annealing and creating balled ends on sterling and fine silver. Check the temperature to see whether your micro torch is hot enough to melt copper; if not, use a propane torch.

PROPANE TORCH

For copper wire, get the hottest torch you can find, such as an inexpensive propane torch from the hardware store. This torch attaches to a small camper's propane tank. Melting copper wire will spit random tiny particles. They cool in the air, but can be unnerving to see. Use protective eye wear to avoid injury.

TILE

You'll want a heat shield to protect your table when torching. A 12-inch (30.5 cm) square ceramic or porcelain tile or a rimmed cookie sheet works great.

CHARCOAL BLOCK OR FIRE BRICK

Use this fireproof surface to quickly anneal multiple wires or a larger surface.

QUENCHING BOWL

This important safety equipment cools the wire and tweezers after torching. Purchase one at most jewelry supply stores or use a metal, glass, or ceramic container you have around the house.

CROSS-LOCKING TWEEZERS

Use these tweezers specially designed for torching to hold your wire.

PROTECTIVE EYEWEAR

Occasionally, metal spits tiny sparks while it melts, and these glasses will protect your eyes.

PICKLE

When heated, sterling silver and copper develop firescale, which darkens the wire and can't be easily removed by polishing. To quickly dissolve the firescale, the metal is bathed in a pickling solution.

quenching bowl

torch

SAFETY TIP

Use caution with pickling solutions. They are highly corrosive, even when stored in a sealed container. Any tools near the container may rust. And always follow the manufacturer's directions when preparing the pickle and disposing of it. As a mom of young kids, I was concerned about exposure to the chemicals. (This is why I work with fine silver, which does not create firescale when torched.) After much research, I decided to go with a slower, but more natural, approach:

Natural pickling solution

Mix 1 cup (240 ml) of white vinegar with 1 tablespoon (18 g) of salt in a plastic container with a lid. This solution can be heated, but it also works cold—it just takes a little longer to clean the metal when cold. This pickle can be stored and when it no longer works, you can dispose of it at your local disposal station. ***note:*** *Because of the heavy metal content, it is not safe to dump down the drain.*

---

finishing tools

LIVER OF SULFUR

I don't feel my jewelry is complete until I patina it. This process brings out the subtle details of the wire and creates contrast. There are three forms of liver of sulfur: solid form, gel form, and premixed solutions. The gel form is the most stable and lasts a long time. Always store it in an airtight container in a dark, cool area.

STEEL WOOL

Use extra-fine (#0000) steel wool to remove the excess patina from the high points of your design, leaving the crevasses dark. Do not use coarser grits because they will scratch the wire; however, extra-fine grit creates a satin finish to your jewelry.

SOFT BRASS WIRE BRUSH

A soft brass jeweler's brush won't leave scratches and adds a nice polish. After using the steel wool, use the brush to remove any steel wool particles caught in the weave.

PRO-POLISH POLISHING PADS AND POLISHING CLOTHS (OPTIONAL)

Use Pro-Polish polishing pads for touch-up work after the steel wool. You can also use polishing cloths to buff the jewelry and give it a glossy finish. *note: I prefer to use a tumbler or a rotary tool with a flex shaft because they are quicker, and I don't risk catching the wire ends with the cloth.*

rotary tumbler

ROTARY TUMBLER (OPTIONAL)

A tumbler creates a beautiful mirror finish on cleaned and polished jewelry. Use a 3-pound (1.36 kg) capacity tumbler with 1 pound (454 g) of stainless steel shot, warm water, and a tiny bit of dishwashing liquid.

ROTARY TOOL WITH A FLEX SHAFT (OPTIONAL)

If tumbling is not an option, use a rotary tool (either an all-purpose Dremel or a professional jeweler's flex shaft) with polishing attachments. Red rouge polishing compound or Scotch-Brite radial bristle disks will create a mirror finish similar to that of the tumbler.

steel wool

polishing cloths

techniques

wireworking tips

Before beginning the projects, develop good habits. This will lead to a higher level of craftsmanship, and the careful attention to details, precision, and consistency will set your jewelry apart. Take the time to practice the techniques, be okay with going slow, and know that with time, you will get faster. The more you work, the more it will become second nature. It takes patience and attention to detail, but the results are well worth it. Creating elegant, refined jewelry starts with the basics. If the base wires are not straight and uniformly spaced, then the woven strip will look hastily done. The same is true for the weave. It's important to strive for neat, precise, and tight wraps within the weave. Every little detail matters.

handling the wire

Your hands are the best tools you have. They tend to be underappreciated and underused. Resist the tendency to always grab for a tool to do the work; your fingers can do a much better job. Remember to take breaks frequently and stretch your hands.

HOLDING SMALL-GAUGED WIRE

A natural tendency is to pinch small-gauged wire between your thumb and forefinger to guide it as you weave, but this will cause your hand to cramp. I use an alternative method inspired by crochet: Instead of pinching the wire, run it across your palm underneath the pinky and across your ring and middle finger

(Fig. 1–3). Allow the wire to run through your fingers while you guide it with your middle finger. Your hand can be open or loosely closed in a fist, as long as you are not clenching the muscles. In the beginning, holding the wire this way may feel awkward. Focus first on learning the weave and holding the wire in a way that feels natural. Once you are comfortable, work on holding the wire using my method.

Another benefit to this method is that I can use my fingers to tap the small-gauged wire to gently tighten it as I'm weaving. This provides the right amount of tension to wrap the wire tightly around the base wires. When my wire is at the back, I tap it with my thumb (Fig. 4). As I move the wire to the front, I use my forefinger to tap it (Fig. 5). Although it's normal to want to use your arm muscles when you pull the wire to tighten it, this actually uses more force than is required and can cause the wire to break. By tapping the wire with your fingers, you use a minimal amount of force to tighten the wire.

PROTECTING YOUR FINGERS

Letting the wire run along your fingers can cause chafing. Use pliable fabric tape to create a buffer between your fingers and the wire. Fabric tape does not restrict movement in your hands.

REDUCING FATIGUE

Holding the base wires can make your hand fatigued and cramp up. A ring clamp fits comfortably in your hands and grips the wire without marring it. Readjust your clamp frequently so that no more than ½ inch (1.3 cm) of the weave is above the clamp. *note: If too much weave is exposed, when you compress the unsupported woven strip it will buckle.*

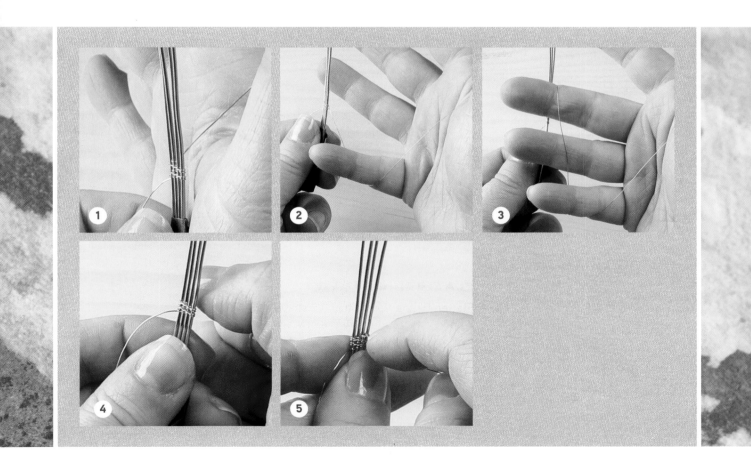

STRAIGHTENING WIRE

Nylon pliers can be used to straighten the wire, but they also compress it, work hardening and slightly flattening it. I prefer to use my fingers instead. Draw the wire between your thumb and index finger, with your thumb pushing against the wire and your index finger slightly above it, guiding the wire. This will cause the wire to arc. Go back to the beginning of the wire, but this time push with your index finger, with your thumb slightly above, guiding the wire. This will arc the wire in the opposite direction. Continue drawing the wire between your thumb and index finger, alternating your finger positions each time. Stop when the wire feels smooth between your fingers. Draw it one more time, and this time press evenly between both fingers. This will straighten the arc. *tip: Use a polishing cloth to protect your fingers as you work.* For stubborn kinks, use flat-nose or chain-nose pliers.

SECURING WIRE

I use painter's tape to keep base wires secure and in the right position when I begin weaving. The tape gives you a wider surface to grip and can help reduce hand fatigue because it allows you to have a gentler grip on the wire. It's easy to remove when finished and doesn't leave a sticky residue like other tapes.

securing shaped base wires

LASHING

I like to tack everything down; I don't want my shaped wires to become undone by a snagged scarf. Similar to coiling, lashing is used to secure, or fasten, two components together. I primarily use it to secure the base wires to each other or to the woven strip. It gives the finished jewelry structural stability. Make sure you are wrapping the smaller-gauged wire tightly around the base wires and that the base wires being lashed are properly secured.

1 Secure the base wires by wrapping two wires together two or three times.

2 Use beads as a way to get from one secured point to the next.

secured wire

3 After securing all the shaped wires, finish the 28g wire by wrapping it around a base wire. Try to find a spot in the back of the jewelry that won't be seen.

SECURING THE 28-GAUGE WEAVING WIRE

The 28-gauge wire needs to be secured before trimming the excess. Do this by wrapping around a base wire two or three times (**Fig. 6**). The smaller the base wire, the better; too large a base (such as 14-gauge) will not secure the 28-gauge wire. Over time, it will unwind. If you have attached a bead with the 28-gauge wire, the best place to secure it is by wrapping around the 28-gauge wire, passing through the bead. After securing the wire, trim it on the back so it's tucked out of the way. *tip: If all else fails, add a bead to create a place to secure the 28-gauge wire to or puncture the weave two rows down and secure the wire as you would in the Woven Stacking Bracelet, page 56.*

puncturing the weave

Use the beading awl to puncture the weave between the base wires. Use the opening to "sew" beads or wire to the weave (**Fig. 7**). Be careful—you'll want a hole just big enough to slip the 28-gauge wire through twice (**Fig. 8**). But, if you push the beading awl in too far, you'll break the weave (**Fig. 9**). If your

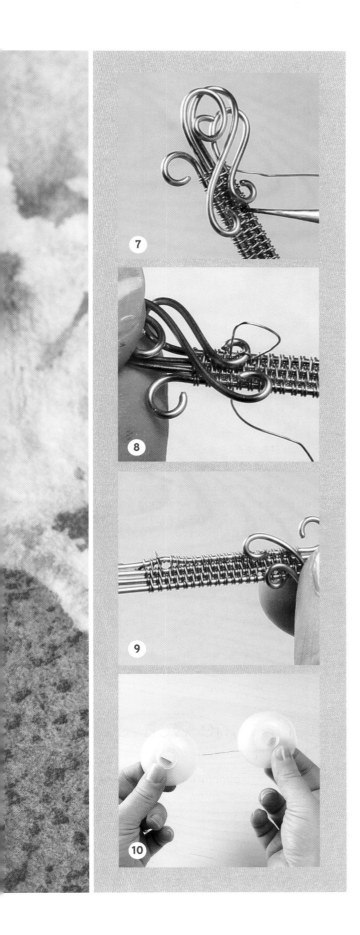

weave does break, trim the loose 28-gauge wires flush to the weave.

preventing tangling and kinks

Preventing kinks eliminates potential weak points in the wire where it's most likely to break. Stop the kinks before they start by being mindful of the wire. If you see the wire looping onto itself, take the time to stop and unloop.

BOBBINS

Traditionally used to make kumihimo braids, these inexpensive bobbins come in several sizes. I like the 1½-inch (3.8 cm) diameter size that fits in the palm of my hand. Starting at the end of the wire, wind smaller gauged wire onto the bobbins and snap the bobbin shut. The closed bobbin has enough tension to keep the wire from raveling, but still allows you to pull out 12 inches (30.5 cm) at a time while weaving. When I am weaving around curves or working with long lengths of wire, I work from the center out **(Fig. 10)**. I use two bobbins and wind both ends to the center of the wire. For example, for 30 feet (9.1 m) of wire, wind 15 feet (4.5 m) onto both to meet at the center. One bobbin becomes your tail; the other is what you are pulling from. When you have finished one side, flip it over. Use the wire on the other bobbin to weave the other half. Use the leftover wire on the spool for smaller projects, so little is wasted.

WORKING FROM THE SPOOL

The wire can uncoil off the spool faster than you can work with it, causing it to tangle. To prevent this, place the spool on the floor while you are working; this stretches the uncoiled wire so it does not tangle on itself. *tip: If your wire came in a coil, take the time to wrap it around a spool or bobbin before working on a project. When purchasing the wire, request it on a spool.* Another option is to use a container just wide enough to hold the spool upright. The spool will spin freely as you work, but not completely uncoil. This can also be done with multiple spools in one container.

annealing

Annealing is done when the wire has been work-hardened and brittle, but still needs further shaping. Heating the wire softens it so it becomes malleable again. I use this technique the most after flattening wire. Annealing can be done on a charcoal block, on a fire brick, or with the cross-locking tweezers holding the wire.

1 Gently heat the length of the wire with the torch, moving the flame back and forth over the wire, being careful not to stay in one spot long enough to begin melting the wire.

2 When the wire surface develops a matte finish and the wire begins to glow, the wire has been annealed. Another way to determine when the wire has reached the appropriate temperature is to mark the wire with a permanent marker. When the mark disappears, the wire is annealed.

3 Allow the wire to air cool for a minute before quenching it in water.

4 You can anneal a woven strip, but I rarely do. If you are not carefully watching the wire, you end up melting your 28g wire before the base wire is annealed.

storing unfinished projects

I do all my prep work before I begin. When I am finished for the night, I wind the small-gauged wire around a bobbin and place the unfinished work with all the loose wires into a zippered sandwich bag in a designated container. I can store multiple projects together without them tangling.

basic weaves

The weave brings all the wires together into a cohesive design. There are many variations of wire weaving, but I like to keep it simple and focus on two types: modified soumak weave and basic figure-eight weave. Each serves a specific purpose and creates a consistent texture.

weaving tips

In the beginning, go slow. Be sure to wrap each base wire tightly with the 28-gauge wire before continuing. This is very important. If you don't, you will end up with a loose, sloppy weave. Stop every time you are perpendicular to the base wires and gently tighten the 28-gauge wire. Yes, this slows you down, but it's worth it. The more you practice, the faster you'll get. At the same time, you'll be amazed at how quickly your weaves improve **(Fig. 11)**.

Another aspect of a tight weave is compression. About every three rows, I stop and compress the weave with my fingernails. This serves two purposes. First, you'll get a consistent and compacted compression of the weave throughout the strip. The goal is not to compress the weave to the point where you can't see the base; that's not possible. Instead, make sure the texture is consistent and even from both left to right and top and bottom. Even if the wire springs up, it will have more consistency. The second reason is to stretch your hands and cut back on fatigue **(Fig. 12)**.

By mixing the different wire gauges, you can achieve an array of design looks and functionality. I like 14- to 20-gauge wires for base wires. When woven, the 18- to 20-gauge is easier to manipulate and shape. The 14- to 16-gauge wires create a sturdy backbone to a woven strip when weaving preshaped wires together. Weave the base wires together with either 28- or 30-gauge wire. By weaving the base wires with more delicate gauges, you create a finely textured and compact weave that lends itself to feminine, dainty jewelry designs.

It can help to pre-oxidize the base wires in the beginning, before you weave. The contrast between the dark base wires and the light weaving wire allows you to better see what is happening. Before you begin

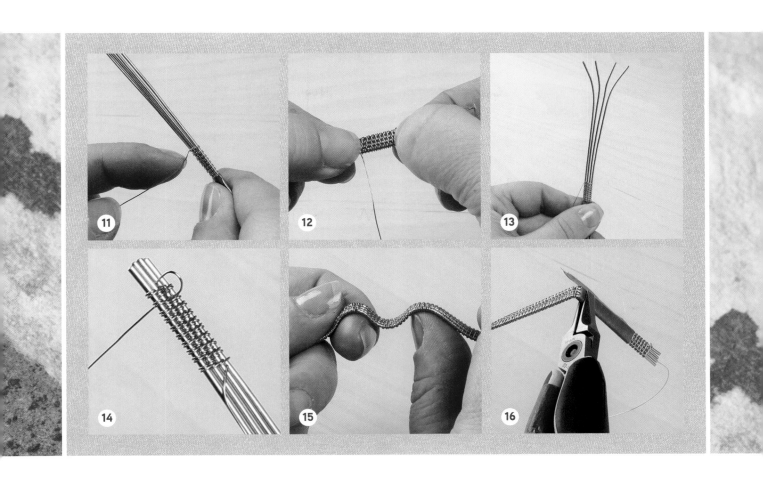

weaving, make sure the wires are properly shaped. Once you start, it will be harder to make adjustments. It's okay to spread the wire apart at the ends, but make sure the base wires are correctly lined up 1 inch (2.5 cm) above the weave **(Fig. 13)**.

When weaving a strip for a bracelet, I like securing my 28-gauge wire in a different method than the normal wrapping around a base wire several times. Stop the weave in the middle of the base wires and with the beading awl, puncture the weave one or two rows down from where you stopped. Wrap the 28-gauge wire around the weave twice and trim. Use flat-nose pliers to tuck in the tail **(Fig. 14)**.

A straight woven strip can be shaped in a variety of ways. For an organic look, use your hands to bend, twist, or gently curve the weave **(Fig. 15)**. For more uniform shaping, use a mandrel. If your fingers are not strong enough to shape the strip against the mandrel, use a rawhide mallet.

forming

Forming adds dimension and depth to the jewelry. You can choose to go subtle or extreme, altering the design and its size. Forming is usually the last thing I do. When possible, I create my woven forms flat because it's easier to achieve symmetry.

Sometimes when forming your woven wire, you will need to use more force, whether it is with a mallet or pliers. However, the small-gauged wire is delicate and must be handled properly. The last thing you want to do is flatten or break the weave. To prevent damaging the weave, cover your weave with painter's tape **(Fig. 16)**.

basic figure-eight weave

This weave is a good one to start with. It's simple and looks good with tight, consistent wraps. Or you can choose to use wraps that are loose and sloppy; this will transform the weave into a rustic, organic style that's also pleasing. This weave is very forgiving as you learn to handle small-gauged wire and make a tidy weave.

The basic figure-eight weave creates grooves or channels between each base wire. These grooves are left dark when patinated, accentuating the shape of the shaped base wires. It can be woven in a strip and then shaped to create a form-fitting bezel, as with the Baroque Pearl Pendant (page 48). It has an organic quality to it, making it my go-to weave when I'm looking for more ebb and flow in a design, or when I want to work freeform.

This weave is also looser than the modified soumak weave because of the gap between the base wires and the fact that when weaving, we move in and out between the spaces of the base wires. (In contrast, in the modified soumak weave, we wrap around each individual wire before moving to the next wire.) This makes it easier to pierce to create open-

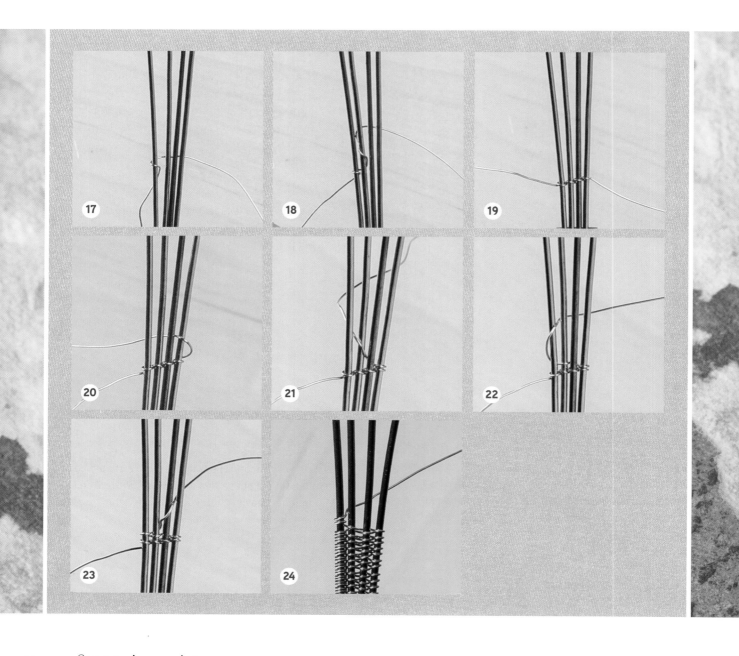

ings for sewing embellishments onto. This weave easily transitions, so you can increase or decrease the number of base wires anywhere in the design.

1   Straighten 16" (40.5 cm) of 18g practice wire and cut four 4" (10 cm) lengths. Tape the 4 wires together at the bottom, leaving a fingernail's distance between each wire. These are the base wires. Cut 5' (152.4 cm) of 28g practice wire; this is the wire used for weaving. The first row is the starter row. It's different from the rest of the weave because it attaches the base wires together. It also stabilizes and positions the base wires. I will refer to the base wires by number, starting on the left with Wire 1, followed by 2, 3, and 4.

2   Leaving a 6" (15 cm) tail, bring the rest of the 28g wire to the back of the base wires. Thread the 28g wire between Wires 1 and 2, and then wrap it around Wire 1, toward the back **(Fig. 17)**. Thread the 28g wire between Wires 2 and 3, and then wrap it around Wire 2, toward the back **(Fig. 18)**. Thread the 28g wire between Wires 3 and 4, and then wrap it around Wire 3, toward the back. Bring the 28g wire across the back of Wire 3 and Wire 4, and then wrap it around Wire 4, toward the back **(Fig. 19)**. Push this starter row down to the base of your thumb. This secures the base wires to each other.

3   It's time to begin weaving. The 28g wire will now be used to weave in and out of the base wires. Starting on the right side, from the back, bring the 28g wire across the back of Wire 4, and wrap it around Wire 4, toward the back. The 28g wire should now be in the back between Wires 3 and 4 **(Fig. 20)**. Bring the 28g wire across the back of Wire 3 and thread it between Wires 2 and 3, toward the front. Take the 28g wire over the front of Wire 2 and thread it between Wires 1 and 2 **(Fig. 21)**. You have reached the end of the row and should be back on the left side of the weave, with the 28g wire in the back.

4   Bring the 28g wire around the outside of Wire 1, toward the front. Thread the 28g wire between Wires 1 and 2, across the back of Wire 2, and then thread it between Wires 2 and 3 **(Fig. 22)**. Bring the wire over the front of Wire 3, thread it between Wires 3 and 4, and then across the back of Wire 4 **(Fig. 23)**. Bring the 28g wire around the outside of Wire 4, and then thread it between Wires 3 and 4,

toward the back. Continue the weave pattern until you reach the left side of the weave, as in Step 3.

VARIATION

Wrap the base wire on the end twice before continuing with the weave. This creates a smoother, more polished line on the edge of the weave, while also thickening the base wire. It's a subtle way of drawing the eye without being obvious. The eye on the Feather Earrings (page 132) stands out because the inner wire was wrapped twice while weaving **(Fig. 24)**.

adding a new weaving wire

Breaks happen. When they do, you don't have to start over. Look at where the break happened. If it is on an outside base wire, undo the weave until you are inside the weave between two base wires, leaving a short tail.

1   Take your new length of 28g wire and insert the tip in the opposite direction of the existing tail. You now have two tails facing opposite directions between the same base wires. Leave enough of a new tail to hold it down with your thumb **(Fig. 25)**.

2   Wrap the new 28g wire once around the base wire before continuing the weave in the original direction you were weaving before **(Fig. 26)**.

3   After you have woven your strip, trim the tails flush. Use flat-nose pliers to tuck the trimmed ends into the weave.

adding a base wire

1   To add a base wire into the weave, spread the existing wires apart where the new wire should be inserted. (In the photo, this is between Wires 2 and 3.) Continue weaving until you have enough space between the separated base wires to comfortably fit the new wire **(Fig. 27)**. *tip: There is no designated spot to add a new wire; add it wherever you can spread the existing wires apart.*

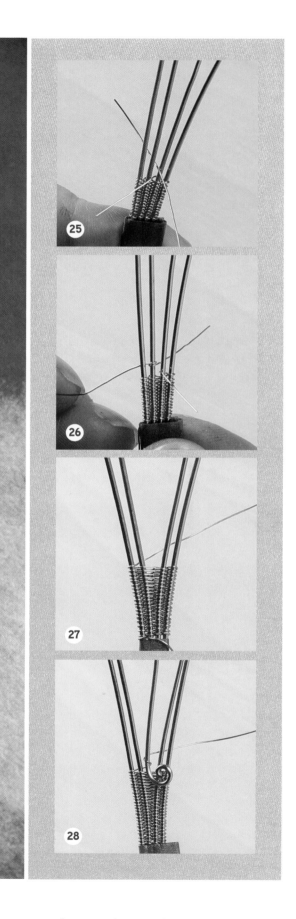

2 Weaving left to right, stop when you reach the new wire. Coming from the back, completely wrap around the new base wire once before continuing the weave. This will secure the new base wire to the other base wires as when we started the weave **(Fig. 28)**.

decreasing the weave

1 To decrease the weave, "drop" a wire from the sides; this means weaving just Wires 1, 2, and 3 together **(Fig. 29)**.

modified soumak weave

This is my favorite weave. When weaving, the goal is to have the base wires as close together as possible, the same width as the small-gauged wire you are weaving with. This weave can be woven into a strip and shaped. Once formed, it holds its shape well. It also works great when weaving shaped wires together. The weave itself creates a tight, uniform texture that does not detract from the overall design. Although it's more complicated than the basic figure-eight weave, it is repetitious. Because the weave is tighter, puncturing the weave when you are adding an embellishment does take a little more strength.

The modified soumak weave has a tendency to zigzag. Compress it frequently with your fingernail to keep the rows straight. A row is weaving left to right, and then right to left, finishing at the starting point. It consists of one row of short wraps and one row of longer wraps.

You can use two or more wires for the base. The more wires you add, the less compact the weave becomes *tip: If the weaving wire breaks, back out of the weave so you are somewhere in the middle of the weave. Insert the new wire between the same two base wires as the broken tail. (The new tail should be going in the opposite direction as the broken tail.) Hold down the tail with your thumb and continue your weave* **(Fig. 30)**. *Trim the tails after you finish the weave* **(Fig. 31)**. *When this weave is done properly, the base wires are only a 28g wire distance apart, so the new 28g wire stays tucked between the base wires without the need for an additional wrap. And, as you compress the weave, it further secures the new 28g wire. If there is too much space between the base wires, it will not hold. If this is the case, wrap around the base wires once before continuing the weave.*

1 Straighten 16" (40.5 cm) of 18g practice wire and cut four 4" (10 cm) lengths. Tape the 4 wires close together at the bottom. These are the base wires. Cut 5' (152.5 cm) of 28g practice wire; this is the wire used for weaving.

LEFT TO RIGHT: BACK ROW

Start by weaving left to right. The base wires are numbered starting on the left with Wire 1, followed by 2, 3, and 4.

2 Leaving a 6" (15 cm) tail, bring the rest of the 28g wire to the back of the base wires, thread it between Wires 1 and 2, toward the front, and then wrap it around Wire 1 in a clockwise direction toward the back **(Fig. 32)**.

3 Bring the 28g wire across the back of Wire 2 and thread it between Wires 2 and 3. Wrap the 28g wire around Wire 2 in a clockwise direction, ending with the 28g wire in the back **(Fig. 33)**.

4 Bring the 28g wire across the back of Wire 3 and thread it between Wires 3 and 4. Wrap the 28g wire around Wire 3 in a clockwise direction, ending with the 28g wire in the back.

5 Bring the 28g wire across the back of Wire 4 and then wrap it around Wire 4 in a clockwise direction, ending with the 28g wire in the back **(Fig. 34)**.

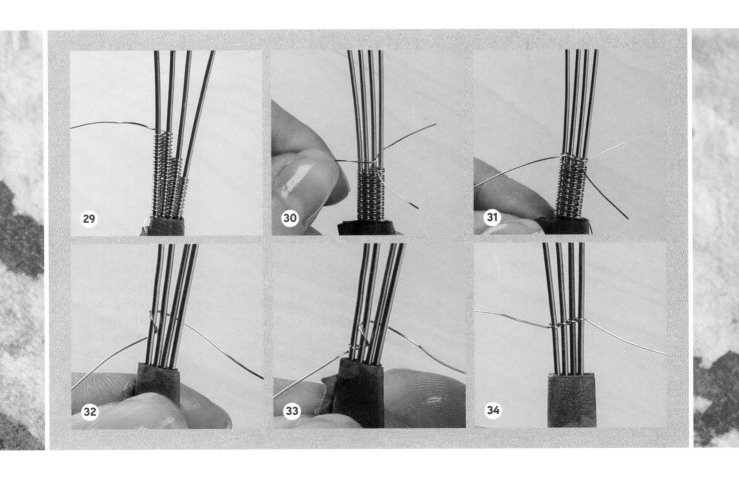

RIGHT TO LEFT: FRONT ROW

You will now be weaving back across the front, right to left. The 28g wire should be in the back, between Wires 3 and 4.

6 Bring the 28g wire across the back of Wire 4 and around the outside of Wire 4 toward the front.

7 Bring the 28g wire over the front of Wires 4 and 3, and then thread it between Wires 2 and 3, toward the back. Wrap the 28g wire around Wire 3 going clockwise, ending on the front, on the right side of Wire 3 **(Fig. 35)**.

8 Bring the 28g wire over the front of Wires 3 and 2, and then thread it between Wires 1 and 2, toward the back. Wrap the 28g wire around Wire 2 going clockwise, ending on the front, on the right side of Wire 2 **(Fig. 36)**.

9 Bring the 28g wire over the front of Wires 2 and 1, and then wrap it around Wire 1 going clockwise. The 28g wire should now be in the front and on the right side of Wire 1 **(Fig. 37)**.

10 You have completed the first row. You should have a row of four short wraps followed by a row of three long wraps. These two rows equal one completed row. Repeat the weave pattern as you did in the beginning, weaving from left to right **(Fig. 38)**.

lashing weave
～

Lashing can be incorporated into a two-base wire weave by alternating coiling with lashing, creating a pleasing pattern. This can be seen in the Kayla Pendant (page 158) and the Petal Bracelet (page 80). It has the added appeal of being a quick weave.

1 Straighten 8" (20.5 cm) of 18g practice wire and cut two 4" (10 cm) lengths. Tape the 2 wires close together at the bottom; these are the base wires. Cut 3' (152.5 cm) of 28g practice wire; this is the wire used for weaving. *note: The left wire will be Wire 1, followed by Wire 2.*

2 Leaving a 6" (15 cm) tail, bring the rest of the 28g wire to the back of the base wires. Coil the 28g wire around Wire 1 twice, making sure that the coils are tight. At the next turn, coil around Wires 1 and 2 two times to lash them together. Coil Wire 2 six times and then lash Wires 1 and 2 twice. Continue the pattern until you reach the desired length **(Fig. 39)**. *note:* *Always coil around one wire before lashing two wires together. This creates a 28g buffer between the base wires.*

braiding

Braiding is a form of weaving the base wires together. See the full instructions in the Baroque Pearl Pendant (page 53).

design elements

Combine these design elements in different ways to create unique jewelry.

loops

SIMPLE LOOPS

1   Trim the excess wire, leaving at least ¼" (6 mm) extra to form the loop. Gently grasp the end of the wire with round-nose pliers **(Fig. 40)**.

2   Rotate the pliers as you press the wire up against the jaw with your thumb. You want your thumb to do the work of shaping the wire as the pliers are rotating, using the jaw of the pliers as a mandrel.

3   Remove the pliers. Use flush cutters to trim the tip of the loop to remove the tool-marked end **(Fig. 41)**. This gives you a perfect circular loop. Notice, using this method you lose the fluid spiral shape achieved when the loops are created by hand.

If you want to close the loop, then reinsert the pliers. While you are barely gripping with the pliers, use your finger to shape the wire around the pliers until the loop is closed.

WRAPPED LOOPS

1   Cut a 3" (7.5 cm) length of 22g wire. Grip the wire about 1¼" (3.2 cm) from one end and make a 90° bend.

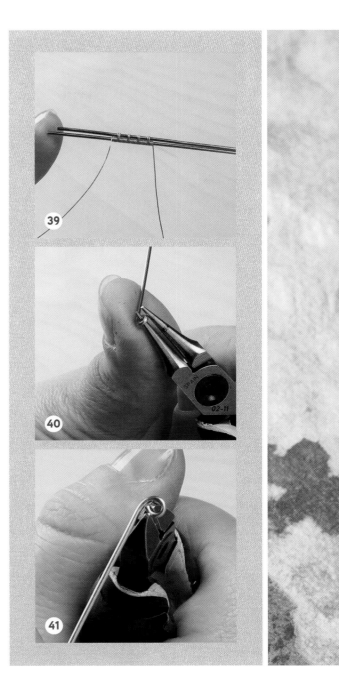

2   Grip the wire at the bend with the round-nose pliers. Shape the 1¼" (3.2 cm) length around the pliers to form a loop with the two arms crossing at or near the 90° bend. Slip the looped end onto the chain. Holding the loop with chain-nose pliers, wrap the shorter arm around the longer arm at the 90° bend. Wrap twice. Trim the wire flush. Use chain-nose pliers to tuck in the trimmed end.

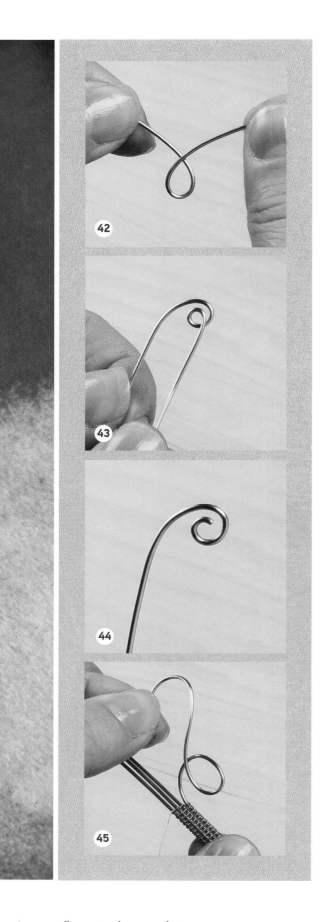

3 Add a bead to the non-looped end and push it down against the wire wraps. With the round-nose pliers, grip the wire above the bead and bend the wire at a 90° angle. Repeat Step 2, but this time, attach the loop onto the pendant.

BRIOLETTE WRAPPED LOOPS

See the Anila Lariat Necklace (page 102) for an example of a finished briolette wrapped loop.

1 Cut an 18" (45.5 cm) length of 24g to 26g wire. Slip the briolette onto the wire with 2" (5 cm) of wire on the left and the remaining wire on the right. Bend the two arms up so that they are parallel and touching.

2 Wrap the 2" (5 cm) arm around the longer arm directly above the bend. Wrap twice and trim. Use the round-nose pliers to create a small loop directly above the wraps. Slip the loop onto the chain or the appropriate opening in the pendant. Holding the loop with the chain-nose pliers, wrap the arm down the existing wraps. Continue to wrap down the briolette, stopping below the briolette's hole. Bring the wire up across all the coiled wraps in the front of the briolette. Wrap the wire around the top just below the loop. Trim the excess wire.

ORGANIC LOOPS

My method of creating organic loops is a signature look for my design style. I use my fingers to create these loops so the wire flows in a unique way. A good example of this type of loop is shown in the Calligraphy Pendant (page 150). You need at least 1" (2.5 cm) of extra wire that will be trimmed after making the loop.

1 Grasp the end of the wire with your fingers and create a "U" shape where you want the loop.

2 Cross the wires over each other to form the loop **(Fig. 42)**.

3 Continue rotating the end of the top wire in a circular motion, closing off the loop. Pull on the end of the wire while creating the circular motion to tighten the loop to the desired size **(Fig. 43)**. *note: All the work of shaping is being done with the end of the wire to create the loop in the center of the wire. Flat-nose pliers can also be used to grip the tip of the wire as you shape.*

4 Trim the excess wire to create a simple loop. Using this method, you can see how the wire is curved slightly in a spiral as you approach the loop, creating a lovely fluid shape **(Fig. 44)**.

LARGE FLOWING LOOPS AND HAND SHAPING

The best way to create flowing, freeform loops or shapes is to move the wire from the end, by hand. By using the wire end, you can guide or lead the wire in the right direction while still maintaining smooth flowing lines. This also allows for more natural movement, creating subtleties that would not have been achieved by forcing the wire with tools to shape a specific spot. I let the wire choose how it wants to bend and move. I am controlling it to a degree, but if it bends in a different manner than expected, I let it. With practice, you will have more control over shaping the wire by manipulating the wire end in different directions **(Fig. 45)**.

Dowels and round-nose pliers can be used as mandrels to help you create consistent loops in the wire before further shaping, as in the Kayla Pendant (page 158). Position the round-nose pliers where you would like to make a large loop, leaving the round-nose pliers open. Grip the end of the wire with your fingers and wrap the wire around the jaw of the round-nose pliers. Remove the pliers and continue to shape the rest of the wire with your fingers.

shaped elements

CREATING "V" SHAPES

1 Mark the wire with a permanent marker where you want the bend.

2 Using flat-nose pliers, gently grasp the wire so you just see the mark on the left side of the pliers. Using your thumb, push the wire away from you and against the pliers at the mark, forming a right angle **(Fig. 46)**.

3 Flip the "V" so the "arm" being held by the pliers is now the arm to be pushed against the pliers. Gently squeeze the arm in the pliers to further straighten it **(Fig. 47)**.

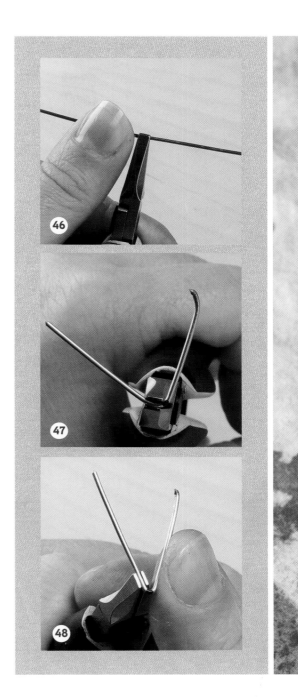

4 Using your thumb, continue to decrease the angle of the "V" to create the desired angle. Rotate the arms frequently as this will create symmetry in the shaping of the "V."

5 Use flat-nose pliers to make sure both arms are straight by gently squeezing each arm with the pliers at the point **(Fig. 48)**.

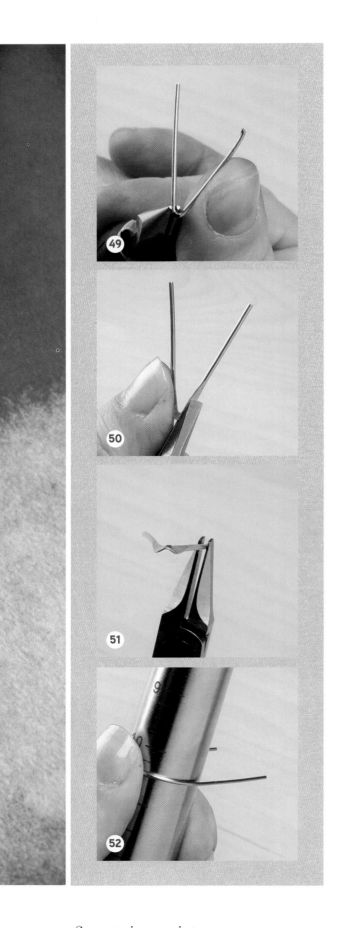

6   If the tip of the pliers is too thick to make a pointed "V" shape, use the chain-nose pliers, and then use the flat-nose pliers to straighten the arms of the "V" **(Fig. 49)**. *note: It's actually easier to use both chain- and flat-nose pliers to make a nice point, but I prefer using one tool instead so I don't have to switch back and forth between tools.*

FOLDING HAMMERED WIRE

I love the look of shaped, flattened wire. However, be careful not to over-flatten the wire, because it can become too brittle and break.

1   Hammer the wire to the desired thickness. Use the micro torch to anneal the wire to soften it.

2   Using flat-nose pliers, grasp the spot you want to fold. Use your thumb to shape the wire over the pliers, forming an angle **(Fig. 50)**.

3   Rotate the wire and grasp the side that was shaped by your thumb in the pliers. Shape the other side, folding it against the pliers. Continue shaping the wire until you create the desired angle, rotating the wire frequently to ensure it's evenly and symmetrically shaped **(Fig. 51)**.

SHAPING CURVES

1   For larger curves, mark the center on the wire where you want the curve to be. Place the wire on the desired ring size of the mandrel.

2   With your thumb positioned over the center mark to keep the wire in place, use your fingers to mold and shape the wire around the ring mandrel from the center out. Only shape one-quarter of the way around the mandrel on both sides, creating a "U" shape **(Fig. 52)**.

3   Stop and make sure the mark is still centered. If it's not, tug the wire on the shorter side, while holding the curved wire to the mandrel with your fingers. This will reposition the wire, without disfiguring the curve **(Fig. 53)**.

4   Continue to shape around the mandrel, alternating between the two sides, until you reach the desired curvature.

5   Place the shaped wire on the bench block. With a rawhide mallet, tap the shape. This will remove any waves that might have happened while shaping.

NESTLING CURVES

When I use my ring mandrel, I drop three sizes down to get a curve that nestles perfectly below the first curve. For example, if the first wire was shaped around the size 10 mark of my mandrel, I would shape the second wire to the size 13 mark **(Fig. 54)**.

CREATING RUFFLES

The goal is to get consistency in shape and length. This comes from practice and knowing how to use the tools. Pointed ruffles are the easiest; curved ruffles require a little more practice.

Pointed Ruffles

The nice thing about pointed ruffles is that you can shape the wire beforehand and then weave it into your design. Pointed ruffles can be made with flat- or chain-nose pliers. Because these pliers taper, mark the pliers with painter's tape before beginning to ensure accuracy. Tear off a small strip of tape and wrap it around the pliers at the desired position. Stick the ends of the tape together to create a flag.

1   Mark the center of the wire to be used for the ruffles. Bend the wire into a 90º angle at the center with the pliers at the marked position. Continue outward, making alternating 90º-angled bends going up one side of the wire. It should look like a zigzag **(Fig. 55)**. When you have made half the ruffles, stop and do the same to the other side. The ruffle is now ready to incorporate into the weave.

2   Attach the ruffles by weaving them into the weave every time the points touch the edge of the base wire. It can be woven in with one row, but for added strength, weave the ruffles into two rows. If you do two woven rows, then the first row should begin just before the point of the ruffle **(Fig. 56)**.

Rounded Ruffles

See the Ruffles and Lace Chandelier Earrings (page 144) for full instructions on how to make rounded ruffles.

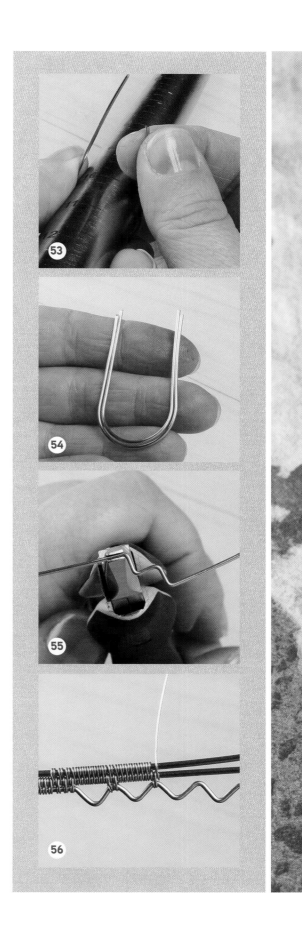

HAMMERING

I love hammering the wire. It transforms wire into a flared, shaped ribbon and adds another layer of texture to the design. Learning to hammer well also adds a more polished, professional look.

To hammer, bring the head down flat onto the wire and then stroke the wire in the direction you want the wire to spread. This motion should be fluid. The stroking motion helps the wire spread in the desired direction and smooths it. You don't need to flatten the wire all at once. As you continue to bring the head down, radiate the strokes out. This helps prevent the wire from overspreading in one direction. Flipping the hammered wire over every few strokes creates a consistent spreading of the wire. If you are experiencing tool marks, then the head is not coming down parallel to the wire. Instead, the edge of the head is hitting the wire, causing the dents **(Fig. 57)**.

PADDLED ENDS

Paddled ends are a great way to end the base wires. No torch is required and it adds a subtle dimension to the design. When paddling, the idea is to create a flared tip.

1   File the wire end flat before hammering; this will cut back on any filing that might be needed afterward.

2   Using a chasing hammer, bring the hammer down flat onto the end of the wire. Move the hammer down the tip in a stroking motion to spread the wire in the desired direction and smooth out any dents. Continue hammering, radiating the strokes out to uniformly flare the tip of the wire. If needed, flip the wire continuously to ensure even hammering on all sides. Be careful not to over-flatten the wire because this will make it brittle and cause it to break.

FLATTENING "V" TIPS

Flattening the tips of the "V" shape adds crispness. When flattening the wire, you want to prevent it from overspreading. The stroking motion should run the length of the tip, instead of radiating out from the wire. This will flatten the wire without too much of a flare in one direction.

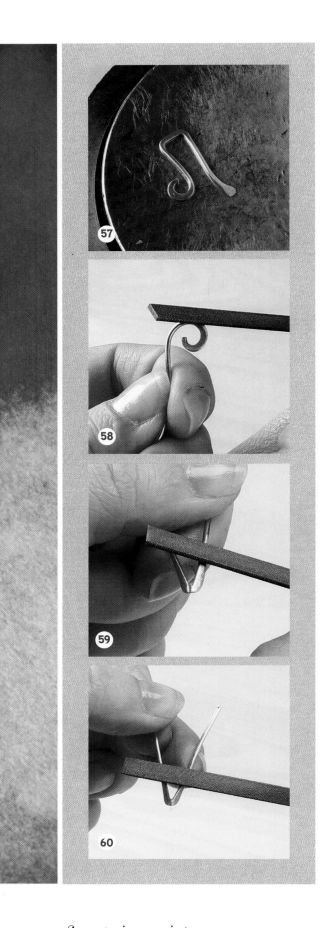

FLATTENING OR FLARING OUT CURVED WIRE

When hammering a curve, you want the wire to gradually spread or flare out more around the curve. This can be the whole curve or just a section, such as a loop.

1 Curve or loop the wire. Using the chasing hammer, begin hammering the curved section, radiating the strokes outward from the wire. As the wire begins to flatten, focus more of the hammered strokes around the areas that you want to flare out more dramatically.

2 It's easy to misshape the curve as you hammer. This happens when you spend too much time hammering in one section of the curve before the rest of the curved wire has been flattened.

FILING

Filing is often the last step in shaping the wire, and it does make a difference in the final product. I find it easier to use needle files or an emery board because it allows me to get into smaller spaces, but a small flat hand file will also work.

BEVELING FLATTENED WIRE

Once the wire has been flattened with the hammer, use a flat file to create a 45º angle along the edge of the flattened wire. This creates a bevel along the edge. I particularly like doing this around flared-out loops and flattened "V" shapes **(Fig. 58)**.

FILING FOLDED WIRE

1 Files can be used to file folded wire into a more rounded shape by smoothing the edges **(Fig. 59)**.

2 Use the file to create a bevel on the inside edge of the fold so that the edge becomes flat **(Fig. 60)**.

ROUNDING FLATTENED ENDS

After paddling the ends of the wire, use the files to round the tip. This is both aesthetically pleasing and brings uniformity to your work **(Fig. 61)**.

TORCHED ELEMENTS

The hottest part of the torch is just in front of the blue flame. To see it better, dim the lights. Always

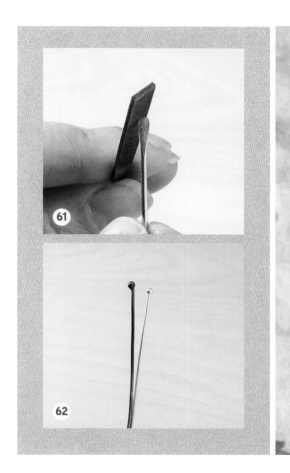

work on a fireproof surface such as a tile and have a bowl of water ready to cool down the wire and tweezers. Cross-locking tweezers are a must, and I prefer working with the longer-tipped ones.

BALLED ENDS

As mentioned previously, copper requires a hotter flame than does sterling or fine silver. Use the appropriate torch for the metal you are working with.

Grasp one end of the wire in the tweezers and hold the tip on the other end perpendicular to the flame. As the wire melts, it will begin to move up the wire, forming a ball. When you have reached the desired ball size, remove the wire from the flame. Let it air cool for a second before "quenching" by placing the wire and tweezers in the bowl of water. Any fast movements made while the ball is still liquid will misshape the ball **(Fig. 62)**.

symmetry

Symmetry requires patience. I spend more time tweaking than I do weaving to ensure that the symmetry is as perfect as I can make it. Here are tips to help you better achieve symmetry:

Center Line

Having a point of reference can help you pinpoint where the symmetry is off. Use a permanent marker to draw a line down the center axis of the design. The mark is not permanent; it will come off after you patinate the jewelry. This line will help you check that all the shaped and woven wires are centered. If they are not, adjust and shape the wires until they are.

Slow Down

It is important to slow down and take your time. It is hard to achieve a symmetrical design while rushing. Step back frequently and look at the whole piece to see whether it is spaced evenly on all sides. Break down the shaping process, so that what you do on one side you immediately do on the other side. If you are getting frustrated, take a break. Things always look and work much better with a fresh perspective and a rejuvenated spirit.

Measure Correctly

One of the easiest ways to mess up on the symmetry is to get the measurements off. Even being ¹⁄₁₆ inch (2 mm) off can skew the symmetry in your jewelry.

Use Dowels

Dowels are a great way to achieve even spacing. Use the desired size to mold the wire around to create bends and curves within the wire or to spread the wires to a consistent distance **(Fig. 63)**.

Check the Back

Sometimes no matter what I do in the front I can't seem to figure out what is causing the lack of symmetry. I know I measured correctly, but I am still off. When this happens, it's time to inspect the back. Sure enough, I find that a wire is bulging or shaped radically differently from what it should be. It's just as important for the back to be symmetrical as it is for the front.

Use Pliers

When using pliers to shape, mark the point where you plan to grip the wire. All flat-, chain-, and round-nose pliers taper. This gives the tools versatility, but it can also throw the symmetry off. Mark the pliers with a permanent marker or with painter's tape **(Fig. 64)**.

finishing touches

Your finished woven component may be embellished in many ways to make it uniquely yours. I love this stage in my classes, as students alter my designs to reflect their own styles. It's the last step before finishing your jewelry and the stage where your jewelry becomes structurally strong and secure.

embellishing

When adding beads to a design, always wrap twice around the base wire before going back through the bead. Wrapping twice locks the bead in place and prevents the 28-gauge wire holding the bead from coming loose **(Fig. 65)**.

coiling

Use coiling to hide the fact that you're trying to get from point A to point B to secure the wires together. When coiling, wrap tightly and frequently compress the coil with your fingers. It's easy to overlap the coils or create uneven spacing, giving the coil a sloppy look. Slow down so that if a mistake happens, you can easily go back and fix it.

finishes

I love to patina my jewelry. Antiquing creates contrast in the woven form, bringing out all the little details and accentuating the depth of the design. Before beginning, wash your jewelry with soap. This removes any oil and residue that occurred from handling it.

USING LIVER OF SULFUR

Many chemicals can create a patina finish. For silver or copper wire, my preference is liver of sulfur. If you can, get liver of sulfur in a gel form. It's easy to use and lasts a long time.

Liver of sulfur works the quickest in hot water (around 130ºF [54.4ºC]). The cooler the water, the longer it takes to oxidize and patina the wire. Wear gloves or use tongs to handle the jewelry while it's in the solution. If the solution gets on your hands, any-

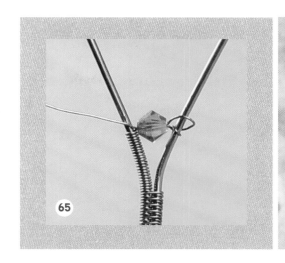

thing silver or copper you touch will start to oxidize. Liver of sulfur has a strong smell and should be used in a well-ventilated area.

To get a deep patina, leave your jewelry in the solution until it has turned a uniform charcoal gray color. For fine silver, this can take longer. Fine silver patinates in a rainbow of colors before reaching the charcoal color. Although these colors are beautiful, I have found when polishing the jewelry that they make the crevasses look dirty instead of antiqued. When you have reached a deep charcoal color, remove the jewelry and soak it in cold water mixed with a couple of teaspoons of baking soda. This neutralizes the liver of sulfur.

Disposing of Liver of Sulfur
To neutralize the liver of sulfur, place the used solution on a windowsill in a sealed jar or in a spot that gets a lot of sun. The sun breaks down the solution. When it has lost its color, it is neutralized and safe to discard. This can be done in the sink, in the toilet, or even in your garden or lawn as a fertilizer. Check locally for any restrictions or alternative methods to dispose of the neutralized solution.

POLISHING

Extra-fine steel wool (#0000) makes polishing simple and easy. If you can't find #0000 steel wool, then a Scotch-Brite pad can be used.

Tear off a small amount of steel wool. Working over a sink, wet the steel wool. Add a little dish soap onto the steel wool and begin to scrub the jewelry. I wet the steel wool for two reasons. First, dry steel wool flakes and leaves steel particles in the air and this is unhealthy to breathe. Second, wetting the wool

fixing & hiding mistakes

Mistakes happen to all of us. It doesn't automatically mean a destroyed design. Here are a few ways to fix, hide, or embrace those flaws:

File the Tool Marks

The best ways to avoid tool marks is to use tools as little as possible. But when tool marks do happen, fix them with needle files. For shallow marks, a light filing is all that is needed. This gives the wire a brushed look. If desired, use fine-grit jeweler's sandpaper to remove the brushed look. For deeper grooves, file the wire to give it a flattened look. Whatever you do, repeat it on the other side to maintain symmetry.

Coil the Base Wire

If you struggle with the shaping, you might rework the wire over and over, mangling it. The best way to cover up these imperfections is to coil the 28-gauge wire over all exposed base wires. This not only hides the imperfections but also gives the design a nice texture.

Anneal the Base Wires

Wire will become brittle and hard as you shape it. The best thing to do is anneal your base wires before working with them. This will soften them and make them easier to reshape. It will also reduce tool marks.

Take a Break

I know it's time to take a break when my wire keeps breaking. Step back, relax, and get rejuvenated. You'll be happier and your jewelry will be better.

Go with the Flow

When a mistake happens in shaping, assembling the wires, or using the improper wire length, it's time to go with the flow. Instead of fighting the wire into submission, modify the design and work around the mistake. Be creative. Maybe adding another layer of shaped wire will balance the mistake or sculpting and molding the woven form differently will make it work. It can be as simple as embellishing with more or different beads to bring it all together.

Mistakes are just new designs waiting to happen. Some of my favorite designs were complete failures that took a new direction. It's an opportunity to step back, think outside of the box, and get very creative. I find I become more adventurous in my designs when mistakes happen. It's already ruined, so why not go extreme and see what becomes of it? The worst that could happen is that I have to start anew; the best is that I end up with an amazing design. For me, that possibility is worth it. At the very least, it is an opportunity to learn and grow.

traps the steel particles in the water and they fall into the sink instead of the air. Adding dish soap increases your productivity, because the patina comes off more easily.

Rinse the soap off the jewelry frequently to ensure you aren't missing any areas. The goal is to remove the patina off the high points while leaving the recesses dark.

When you have finished polishing, use a soft brass wire bristle brush or toothbrush to scrub the jewelry all over. This removes any steel wool caught in the jewelry. Rinse the jewelry again and dry. Use a Pro-Polish pad on any areas missed by the steel wool and to create a nice shine on the high points.

CREATING A MIRROR FINISH

You can leave the jewelry as is after removing the patina for a satin finish. But for a mirror finish polish, use one of these methods:

Tumbling

This is my favorite and the easiest way. Use a 3-pound (1.36 kg) tumbler with 1 pound (454 g) of mixed stainless steel shot and a drop of Dawn dish soap. The shot acts like tiny hammers and smooths the wire surface. Tumble for 30 minutes or several hours without damage to the jewelry. The tumbler blends the transitions from light to dark within your jewelry.

Be careful of the stones and crystals you put in the tumbler. They should have a hardness of at least 7 on the Mohs scale. Instead of tumbling with stones, gems, crystals, or pearls, I add embellishments after I tumble. Avoid tumbling more than one chain to prevent a tangled mess.

Pro-Polish Pad or Polishing Cloth

This inexpensive option gives the jewelry a nicer polish than the satin finish from steel wool. However, the polish is not as nice as the one from a tumbler or flex shaft, my preferred methods.

Soft Brass Wire Bristle Brush

Scrubbing with a jeweler's soft brass wire bristle brush over your jewelry gives it a higher polish than steel wool does. It's not as good as a tumbler, but it's still an excellent and simple option. Do not buy cheaper brass wire bristle brushes at hardware stores because these will scratch the surface instead of polishing it.

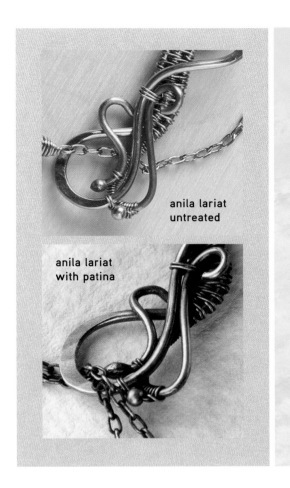

anila lariat untreated

anila lariat with patina

Dremel Flex Shaft or Rotary Tools

I use this method only when tumbling is not an option. Before you begin polishing, tape the chain down onto a discarded piece of wood. If you don't, you risk the chain getting caught in the shaft and destroying your jewelry.

The felt attachments for polishing do not work with woven forms. Instead, use a leather buffing wheel. It holds up better, making it worth the extra money. Use red rouge to polish the jewelry on a low setting. When you're finished, scrub the jewelry with soap and a toothbrush to remove the rouge compound. I have also found that the Scotch-Brite radial bristle disks work really well.

findings

Making your own findings adds a personal touch to your finished jewelry; it shows that you have thought about every detail. I go out of my way to keep only a few lobster-claw clasps and post earrings on hand.

This forces me to get creative and find artistic yet functional ways to design findings that meld well with my jewelry.

head pins

Most projects use a torch to create balled ends for head pins. If you prefer not to use a torch, you can create paddled head pins using wire heavier than 20g and a hammer. See page 32 for tips on hammering.

ball-end head pins

MATERIALS AND TOOLS

3" (7.5 cm) of 20g wire

Tile

Protective eyewear

Butane micro torch

Cross-locking tweezers

Quenching bowl

Needle files

Chasing hammer

Steel bench block

Permanent marker

Ruler

Wire cutters

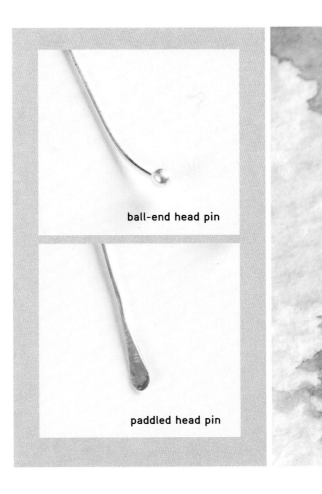

ball-end head pin

paddled head pin

1   Place a tile on your work surface. With the torch, and wearing protective eyewear, ball one end of a 3" (7.5 cm) piece of wire. *note: To make two identical head pins, cut two 3" (7.5 cm) pieces of wire.*

2   Holding the wire with cross-locking tweezers. Quench.

ear wires

spiral post ear wires

spiral post ear wires

Use these ear wires in the Ruffles and Lace Chandelier Earrings (page 140).

MATERIALS AND TOOLS

6" (15 cm) of 20g wire

Ruler

Wire cutters

Needle files

Permanent marker

Chasing hammer

Steel bench block

Flat- or chain-nose pliers

1   Cut two 3" (7.5 cm) pieces of 20g wire. File the ends. Mark one end ½" (1.3 cm) in. Hammer the entire length of the wire except the ½" (1.3 cm) on the end.

2   Anneal the wire. With the flat-nose pliers, grip the wire at the ½" (1.3 cm) mark and begin to spiral the wire. Continue to roll the wire onto itself along the flattened side of the wire **(Fig. 66)**.

3   Stop when you have 1" (2.5 cm) of wire left.

4   Hold the end of the wire below the spiral with the tip of the flat- or chain-nose pliers. Bend the wire toward the spiral **(Fig. 67)**.

5   Finish spiraling the last bit of wire so it stops somewhere on the top. File the ends smooth.

french ear wires
with a twist

Add these ear wires to the Feather Earrings (page 132) for the perfect finishing touch.

MATERIALS AND TOOLS

6" (15 cm) of 20g wire

Ruler

Wire cutters

Needle files

Chasing hammer

Steel bench block

Round-nose pliers

Flat-nose pliers

1   Cut two 3" (7.5 cm) pieces of 20g wire. File and hammer one end. Curl the paddled tip into a small loop. *tip: If you are finding this difficult, anneal the wire.*

2   Grip the wire below the loop with the base of the round-nose pliers. Form the wire around the pliers and bring the wire up next to the loop **(Fig. 68)**.

3   Holding the wire above the loop with the flat-nose pliers, bend the wire at the top of the pliers in a wide angle away from the loop **(Fig. 69)**.

4   At the new bend, grip the wire with the base of the flat-nose pliers. Bend the wire in a 90º angle. Reposition the base of the pliers on the other side of the 90º bend. Bend the wire in a wider angle. The top of the ear wires should look like a diamond.

5   Curve the end of the wire starting at the last bend to form a gentle concaved arc. Trim the end to the desired length.

6   File the trimmed end. Hammer the top of the ear wires and the filed tip.

french ear wires

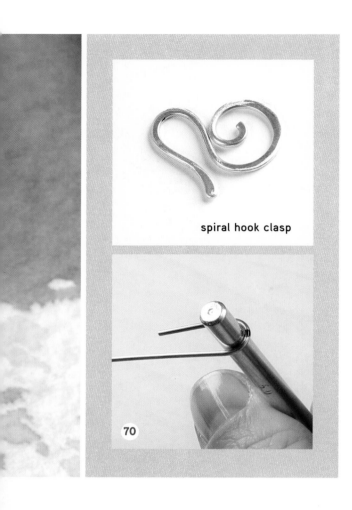

spiral hook clasp

70

spiral hook clasp
〜

This simple clasp makes a nice alternative to the S-clasp.

MATERIALS AND TOOLS

3" (7.5 cm) of 16g wire

Ruler

Wire cutters

File

Permanent marker

5mm dowel

Round-nose pliers

Chasing hammer

Steel bench block

1 Cut one 3" (7.5 cm) piece of 16g wire. File one end and mark the wire ½" (1.3 cm) from this end.

2 Bend the marked end around a 5mm dowel, forming a "U" shape with the ½" (1.3 cm) mark centered on the "U" **(Fig. 70)**. Curve the shorter arm out with the round-nose pliers to form a tail.

3 Grip the tip of the longer wire arm with the round-nose pliers. Loosely spiral the end downward and in toward the ½" (1.3 cm) mark, for a full turn and a half, forming a spiraled "S" shape. Trim the tool-marked end.

4 Place the clasp onto a steel bench block. Use the chasing hammer to paddle the wire tail and flare out the curves in the clasp. Use the file to round the paddled tail end and bevel the hammered curved sections.

decorative s-clasp

Use this stunning clasp in the Kayla Pendant (page 158). For a simpler S-clasp, such as the one used in the Calligraphy Pendant (page 150), follow the first two steps of these instructions.

MATERIALS AND TOOLS

4" (10 cm) of 14g sterling silver wire

6" (15 cm) of 18g fine silver wire

3' (91.5 cm) of 28g fine silver wire

1 sterling silver 4mm round

1 sterling silver 3mm round

Flat needle file

Ruler

Fine-point permanent marker

Steel ring- sizing mandrel

Round-nose pliers

Chasing hammer

Steel bench block

Painter's tape

Beading awl

Liver of sulfur

#0000 fine steel wool

Soft brass wire bristle brush or toothbrush

Pro-Polish pad or polishing cloth

Rotary tumbler with mixed stainless steel shot (optional)

cutting and forming the wire

1   File both ends of the 14g wire flat. Mark both ends 1¼" (3.2 cm) in with the permanent marker. Bend one end of the wire around the tip of the ring mandrel, creating a "U" shape, centering the 1¼" (3.2 cm) mark in middle of the "U." Bend the other end of the wire around the tip of the ring mandrel in the opposite direction, creating an "S" shape.

2   Compress the curves between your fingers, creating an organic oval shape. Using round-nose pliers, bend the ends of the wire outward **(Fig. 71)**. Use the chasing hammer and steel bench block to paddle the ends of the wire and the curved sections (see Hammering, page 32). Round the paddled ends with the file. If making the Decorative S-Clasp, continue to Step 3.

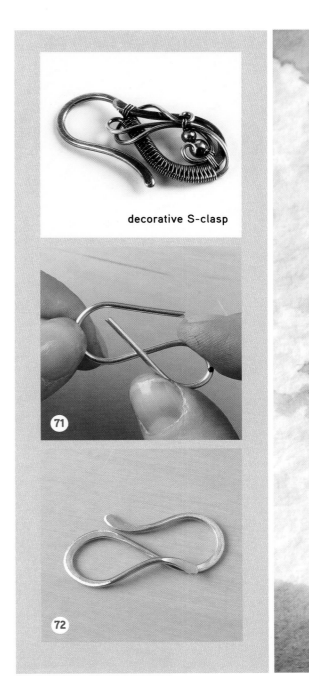

decorative S-clasp

If making the Simple S-Clasp, bevel the edges of the curve and push the bottom tail up over the middle arm. With your fingers, form the clasp into a gentle dome to finish the Simple S-Clasp **(Fig. 72)**.

3   Mark the center of the 18g wire.

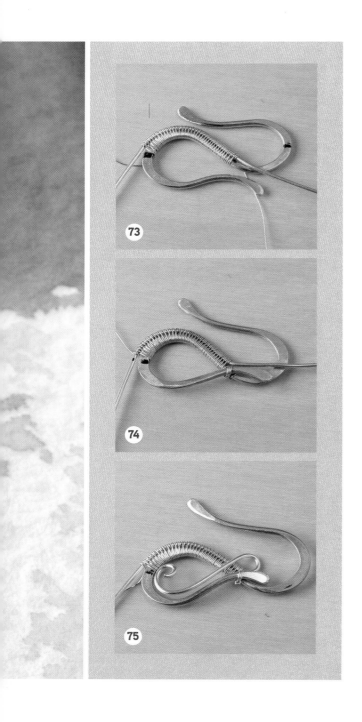

73

74

75

weaving

4 Place the clasp on the ruler with the bottom curve on the left. Re-mark the center line in the bottom curve if it's not visible. Mark the middle "arm" of the clasp ⅞" (2.2 cm) from the center mark on the bottom curve.

5 Line up the center mark on the 18g wire with the center mark on the bottom curve. Bend the 18g wire around the curve and along the outside of the middle arm, crossing the end of the 18g wire over the 14g wire.

6 Tape the bottom half of the 18g wire to the bottom arm. Leaving a 6" (15 cm) tail, use the 28g wire to weave the 18 and 14g wires together, using the modified soumak weave (page 24). Begin at the center mark on the bottom curve and weave to the ⅞" (2.2 cm) mark on the middle arm. Remove the tape **(Fig. 73)**. Using your fingers, push the bottom tail over the upper arm at the ⅞" (2.2 cm) mark; lash the tail to the upper arm (see Lashing, page 18). **(Fig. 74)**

7 There is enough room between the lashes to thread the 28g wire through to secure the wire. Trim the excess.

shaping the 18g wire

8 Starting at the ⅞" (2.2 cm) mark, bend the 18g wire up and around. Cross the 18g wire over the weave. Using your hands, shape it so it curves along the inside of the bottom tail and the curve of the 14g wire, stopping at the center mark.

9 Form an organic loop with the shaped 18g wire just above the center mark and trim (see Organic Loops, page 28). **(Fig. 75)**

10 Take the bottom half of the 18g wire and curve it over the 14g wire, the shaped 18g wire, and the weave, ending up on the left-hand side of the loop in the 18g wire.

11 Wrap the 18g wire around the back of the weave and over the bottom tail. Create an organic loop, swirling the loop out, over the 18g wire at the bottom of the curve. Trim **(Fig. 76)**.

12 With the beading awl, create a space between the 18g wire and the 14g wire at the center mark. This is where you will attach the chain with a link or jump ring **(Fig. 77)**.

13 Lash the looped 18g wire to the 14g wire at the center mark. Thread one 4mm and one 3mm round onto the 28g wire. Cross it under the top 18g wire and lash the second loop to the top 18g wire. Thread the 28g wire back through the round, wrap once around the 18g wire, and secure the 28g wire. Trim **(Fig. 78)**.

14 With your fingers, form the clasp into a gentle dome.

finishing touches

15 Oxidize with liver of sulfur if desired. Polish with the steel wool and brass brush. Use the Pro-Polish pad or polishing cloth to add shine to the high spots or tumble in the rotary tumbler.

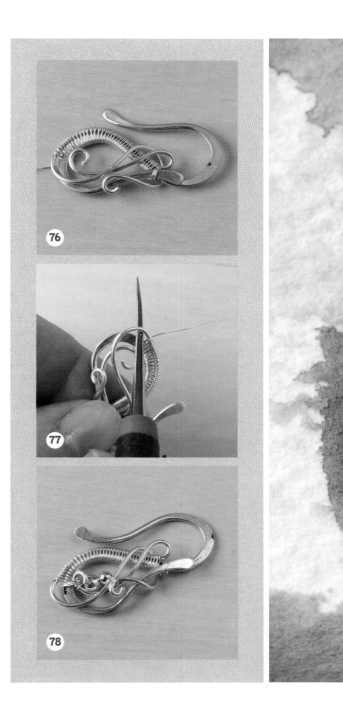

projects

TECHNIQUES

Basic Figure-Eight Weave (page 22)

Braiding (page 53)

Adding a Base Wire (page 23)

Decreasing the Weave (page 24)

Puncturing the Weave (page 18)

Forming (page 21)

Loops (page 27)

Lashing (page 18)

MATERIALS

29" (73.5 cm) of 20g fine silver wire

7' (213 cm) of 28g fine silver wire

1 white side-drilled Biwa pearl, 22x7.5mm

15½" (39.5 cm) of sterling silver

1mm chain with attached spring-ring clasp

TOOLS

Ruler

Flush cutters or wire cutters

Needle file

Round-nose pliers

Flat-nose pliers

Painter's tape

Fine-point permanent marker

Beading awl

Liver of sulfur

#0000 extra-fine steel wool

Soft brass wire bristle brush or tooth-brush

Polishing cloth (optional)

Tumbler (optional)

baroque
pearl
PENDANT

This is the pendant that started it all. Looking back, it is thrilling to see how such a simple design helped unlock my potential. I remember being so excited when I finished. What makes this a great project for beginners is that it looks amazing even if your weave is far from perfect. The loose, uneven weave will give the pendant an earthy quality that lends itself well to the organic nature of the pendant.

level ⟹ **BEGINNER**

finished size ⟹ ¼" wide x 1¾" high (6 mm x 4.5 cm)

length ⟹ 15½" (39.5 cm)

Because the woven strip is shaped around the bead, your design options are limitless. Have fun mixing it up by using oddly shaped beads, as those meld beautifully with this design.

cutting and forming the wire

1 Cut two 4" (10 cm) pieces of 20g wire. File one end of each wire flat. Using round-nose pliers, create a simple loop on the filed end. Using your fingers, spiral the loop for half a turn.

2 Cut three 7" (18 cm) pieces of 20g wire. Bend one wire in half with your fingers, forming a "U" shape. Cross the wire arms to form a loose loop. Continue to bend the top arm around to tighten the loop. Bring that arm all the way around, stopping when the two arms are parallel. Set aside **(Fig. 1)**.

3 Using the back of the round-nose pliers, bend the last two 7" (18 cm) wires in half to form a "U" shape 3 mm wide. Using flat-nose pliers, gently squeeze one of the wires at the bend until it fits inside the first wire, leaving enough room for the 28g wire to loosely fit between each arm. Tape the wires together at the bend, covering ¼–½" (6mm–1.3 cm) of the wires. You now have four base wires to weave together. Orient the wires so the "U" shapes are at the bottom. The wires will now be referenced by number. The first wire on the far left is Wire 1, followed by Wires 2, 3, and 4.

weaving

4 Leaving a 6" (15 cm) tail, use 6' (183 cm) of the 28g wire to weave the four base wires together using the basic figure-eight weave, starting the weave ½" (1.3 cm) from the bottom of the outer "U." Weave for four rows.

5 Remove the tape and push the weave down the base wires, stopping ⅛" (3 mm) from the end of the outer "U" shape. Pull the inner wires so the inside "U" butts up against the weave, creating a gap between the two U-shaped ends of the wires. Coil the outer U-shaped wire with the 6" (15 cm) tail until all the exposed wire is covered. Trim the excess 28g wire flush **(Fig. 2)**.

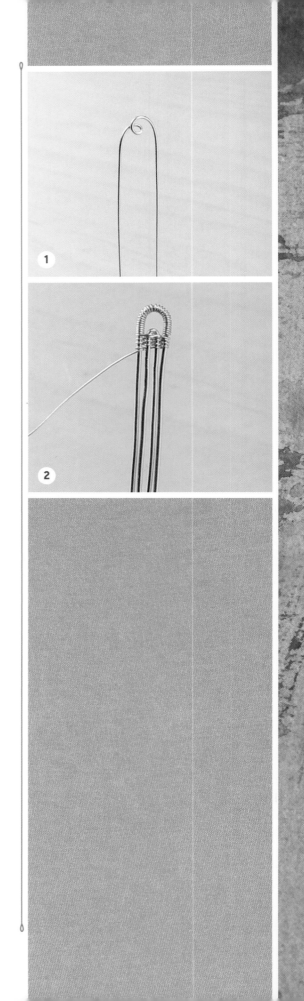

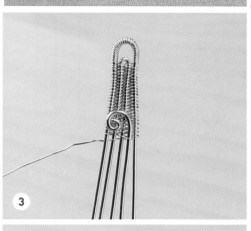

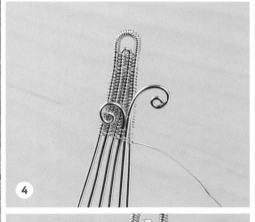

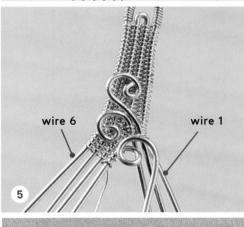

wire 6   wire 1

6 Position the weave right-side up and use the permanent marker to mark Wire 1 at ¾" (2 cm) from the bottom of the outer U-shaped wire. Separate the four wires so Wire 1 is by itself on the left and Wires 2, 3, and 4 are on the right; there should be a gradual opening between Wires 1 and 2, leaving just enough room to add another base wire at the ¾" (2 cm) mark.

7 Continue weaving until you get to the ¾" (2 cm) mark, maintaining the gap between Wires 1 and 2.

adding base wires

8 At the ¾" (2 cm) mark, increase the weave by placing one of the looped wires from Step 1 between Wires 1 and 2 as shown **(Fig. 3)**. *note: You will now be weaving five base wires together.* Continue weaving for two rows with Wire 1 still off to the left. As you come around to the third row, add the second looped wire between Wire 1 and the first looped wire just added. The second looped wire should sit below the first looped wire, and the two loops should face in opposite directions. Weave all six base wires together for two more rows before stopping the weave on the right **(Fig. 4)**.

9 Separate the base wires in the middle. The wires will now be renumbered and referenced as follows: starting on the outside left are Wires 1, 2, and 3, followed by Wires 4, 5, and 6 on the right. Weave Wires 4, 5, and 6 together for two rows. Add the last 7" (18 cm) wire set aside in Step 2 to the center of the base wires. Position the loop of the 7" (18 cm) wire in the center where Wires 3 and 4 are separated, with the top arm of the loop on the left and the bottom arm on the right **(Fig. 5)**.

10 There should now be four wires on the left and four wires on the right. You will be weaving the four wires on the right together until you have reached three-fourths of the length of the pearl. *tip: Because this exact spot depends on the size and shape of the focal bead you are using, it helps to line up the bead to the wires and mark where you need to stop before beginning to weave the four wires together.*

braiding

11 Make any final adjustments to the two loops from Step 9 over the weave so their orientation and shape is pleasing to you. *tip: This step is an excellent place to put your own personal touch on the design. Shape, shorten, lengthen, or rotate the loops as you please.* Braid the remaining four wires together for the length of the pearl. See page 53 for instructions on braiding. Compress the braid to make it uniform and then twist the braid so it lies flush against the pearl with the center bumps of the braid on the outside **(Fig. 6)**.

forming the weave

12 Using your fingers, form the woven strip so it molds around the pearl **(Fig. 7)**. As you are forming the weave, rotate it slightly to create a nice bezel around the edge of the pearl, adding depth.

13 From where you left off in Step 10, decrease the weave, weaving around only Wires 6, 7, and 8 for several rows. Decrease the weave again, weaving around only Wires 7 and 8, until you have woven the length of the pearl.

connecting the weave with the braid

14 Twist Wires 5 and 6 together in a counterclockwise direction for one turn **(Fig. 8)**. Check the fit of the pearl to ensure that it still fits properly inside the bezel. Join the wires of the woven side with the wires from the braided side by crossing the wires over and under each other in a random manner. *tip: You don't have to use all the wires, but enough so they are locked into place and won't come apart if you pull them. Sometimes all I need is three wires crossing over each other to join the two sides; other times I cross all the wires over and under each other.* When I am joining the two sides, I begin to think about where I want my swirls and will cross wires over to also get them into position to be further shaped **(Fig. 9)**.

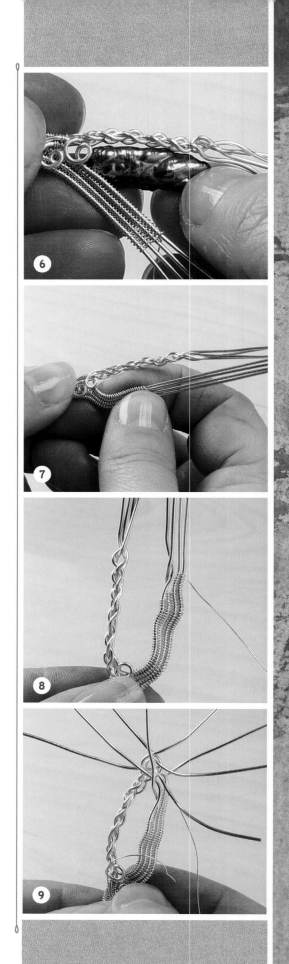

how to braid wire

If you are creating a braid for a different project, you'll need to first weave 1" (2.5 cm) of the four base wires together with 28g wire using any weave you like.

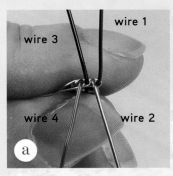

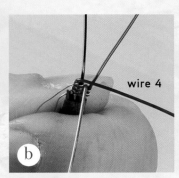

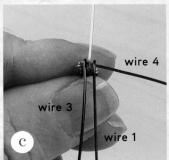

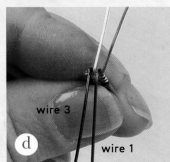

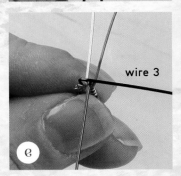

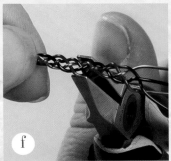

1 Tape the four wires close together at the bottom.

2 With your fingers, push Wires 1 and 3 up and Wires 2 and 4 down (**Fig. A**).

3 Bend Wire 4 horizontally across the remaining three wires. Wires 1 and 3 should be above Wire 4, and Wire 2 should be below Wire 4 (**Fig. B**).

4 Bend Wires 1 and 3 down over Wire 4 and bend Wire 2 up over Wire 4. There should be no wires crossing over any other wires except for Wire 4 (**Fig. C**).

5 Push Wire 4 up parallel to Wire 2 (**Fig. D**). You should be back to two wires up and two wires down.

6 Bend Wire 3 across Wire 2, above Wire 1, and across Wire 4 (**Fig. E**). Repeat the pattern to braid the desired length (**Fig. F**). *note: The braid does not have to be very tight. The uniformity comes when it's compressed in Step 7.*

7 Compress the braid with flat-nose pliers to give it a uniform look (**Fig. G**).

15 Trim the wire ends to the desired length. Make the loops and swirls with the round-nose pliers in a pattern that is pleasing to you and then trim the excess wire. *tip: This is a great place to practice making organic loops. I like making a mix of small loops with a little swirl near the braid followed by longer swirls of wire going up the woven side.* File the ends smooth after you have trimmed the wire. Using round-nose pliers, create simple loops on the wire ends.

16 Use the extra 28g wire still attached to the weave to anchor the loops and keep them from pulling loose. We do this by threading the 28g wire up from the back to the point where a loop needs to be secured and lashing the loop to a neighboring loop or base wire. Thread the 28g wire through the joined section to bring it to the back; staying in the back, hop over to the next loop that needs to be secured. Secure the 28g wire by wrapping around a base wire in the back three times and then trim the excess wire **(Fig. 10)**.

creating the bail

17 Using the back of the round-nose pliers, gently bend the U-shaped top of the pendant toward the back as shown **(Fig. 11)**.

securing the focal pearl

18 Oxidize the pendant, chain, and remaining 12" (30.5 cm) of 28g wire with liver of sulfur before adding the pearl. Polish with the steel wool and brass brush. Use a polishing cloth or a tumbler to clean and brighten the jewelry.

19 String the pearl onto the center of the 12" (30.5 cm) 28g wire. *tip: Use the remaining 12" (30.5 cm) of 28g wire if the leftover 28g wire is too work-hardened to use.* Find where the pearl hole lines up with the weave and use the beading awl to puncture the weave at that spot. Attach the pearl by threading the 28g wire through the puncture in the weave on one side and through an opening in the braid. Continue to zigzag the 28g wire on the back of the pearl, alternating from the braid to the weave. This will secure the pearl tightly to the pendant. Secure the 28g wire by either wrapping around a base wire three times in the back or by wrapping around the 28g wires holding the pearl in place; trim **(Fig. 12)**. *note: This step can also be done before you oxidize.*

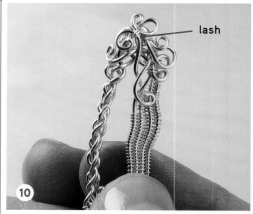

lash

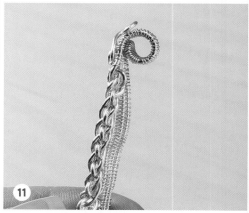

back view

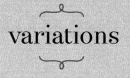

variations

Use a rounded briolette labradorite stone with silver wire to create this variation below.

Another idea is instead of braiding, add a new length of 28g wire and weave the other side. Bring the two sides together in the same manner as you would if it had been braided.

TECHNIQUES

Modified Soumak Weave (page 24)

Puncturing the Weave (page 18)

Hammering (page 32)

Forming (page 21)

Loops (page 27)

Beveling Flattened Wire (page 33)

Annealing (page 20)

MATERIALS

14" (35.5 cm) of 14g dead-soft sterling silver wire

9½" (21.5 cm) of 16g dead-soft sterling silver wire

28" (71 cm) of 18g dead-soft sterling silver wire

30' (9.1 m) of 28g fine silver wire

TOOLS

Ruler

Flush cutters or wire cutters

Fine-point permanent marker

Painter's tape

2 bobbins

Beading awl

Needle file

Round-nose pliers

Flat-nose pliers

Chasing hammer

Steel bench block

Charcoal block or fire brick

Protective eyewear

Cross-locking tweezers

Butane micro torch

Quenching bowl

Rawhide mallet

Bracelet mandrel

Tile

Liver of sulfur

#0000 extra-fine steel wool

Soft brass wire bristle brush or toothbrush

Polishing cloth (optional)

Tumbler (optional)

woven
STACKING BRACELET

Practice the modified soumak weave and turn the strip into a fashionable stacking bracelet. The articulated clasp adds a simple way to finish the bracelet that complements the style.

level ⇒ **BEGINNER**

length ⇒ 7½" (19 cm)

cutting and marking the wire

1 Cut four 7" (18 cm) pieces of 18g wire, making sure that the wires are straight. Mark the center of each wire with the permanent marker. Tape the four wires together at the mark.

2 Wind the ends of the 30' (9.1 m) of 28g wire onto two bobbins so they meet in the center, with 15' (4.5 m) of wire on each bobbin.

weaving

3 Take one bobbin in hand and begin weaving the four wires together using the modified soumak weave. Make sure that the base wires are straight and only have a gap between them the size of the 28g wire. Stop weaving ¼" (6 mm) from the end of the base wires, in the center of the base wires.

4 Cut the 28g wire, leaving a 4" (10 cm) tail. Using the beading awl, puncture the weave one row down between the center base wires and thread the 28g wire through the hole in the weave as shown. Wrap the 28g wire tail twice around the row. Trim the 28g wire flush on the back of the bracelet.

5 Trim the base wires to the same length and file the ends flat **(Fig. 1)**.

6 Push one base wire toward the back of the weave. Using round-nose pliers, create a simple loop with the loop facing the back of the weave, making sure the loop is big enough for the 16g wire to fit through. Repeat with the remaining three base wires **(Fig. 2)**. *tip: After the first simple loop is made, the looped wire will get in the way of the pliers when you try to loop the next wire. Insert the nose of the round-nose pliers through the previous loop to finish making the new loop.*

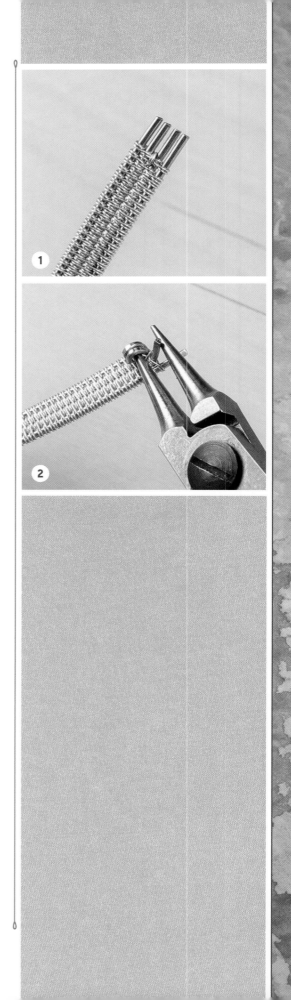

7 Remove the tape and weave the second half of the bracelet. Stop weaving ¼" (6 mm) from the end of the base wires, stopping in the center of the base wires.

8 Repeat Steps 4–6.

making the clasp and pins

9 Cut 3" (7.5 cm) of 16g wire and mark the center with the permanent marker. Cut 3½" (9 cm) of 16g wire and mark the center. Cut two 1½" (3.8 cm) pieces of 16g wire and mark each of these wires ½" (6 mm) from one end.

10 Line up the center of the 3" (7.5 cm) wire in the back of the flat-nose pliers. Using your fingers, bend both ends of the wire down around the bottom jaw of the pliers, creating two 90º angles **(Fig. 3)**.

11 Cut the ends of the wire 1⅛" (2.8 cm) down from the bend and file the ends. Use the chasing hammer and steel bench block to hammer the shaped end, ¼" (6 mm) up from the bend on each side. *tip: If you would like, you can bevel the flattened outer edges with the files for a more refined look.* Make a mark on the jaws of the round-nose pliers with the permanent marker to use as a guide for creating a loop large enough to freely spin around a 16g wire. This will ensure your loops are consistent in size. Create a simple loop at the ends of the U-shaped wire, with the loops facing the same direction and looped to the back of the clasp. Thread a piece of 16g wire through the loops to make sure the clasp hangs straight and the 16g wire has room to spin.

12 Using flat-nose pliers, bend the 3½" (9 cm) wire at the center mark to form a tight "V' shape. Hammer the tip of the "V." Place the charcoal block on the work surface and put on the protective eyewear. Use the micro torch to anneal the "V" on the V-shaped wire so it will be easier to bend into a hook shape later on. Quench.

13 Mark each "arm" of the V-shaped wire ⅜" (1 cm) from the point of the "V." Grasp one arm of the "V" to the right of the mark with flat-nose pliers, as shown, with the tip of the "V" on the right **(Fig. 4)**. Using your fingers, bend the section of wire on the left of the pliers around the nose of the pliers to form half of the hook. Create a matching bend on the other side to complete the hook.

14 Straighten the arms of the hook with flat-nose pliers so they are spread apart and not crossing each other. Insert the hook into the other half of the clasp as shown to make sure it fits properly. Adjust the angle of the hook if needed.

15 Cut the wire arms 1⅛" (2.8 cm) down from the hook and file the ends flat. Using the mark you made on the round-nose pliers as a guide, create a simple loop on the end of each arm, with the loops going toward the hook (**Fig. 5**). *tip: If you would like, you can use the file to bevel or round the flattened sections of the hook.*

16 Using flat-nose pliers, bend each 1½" (3.8 cm) wire at the mark, forming a 90º angle. These will be the pins.

making textured bands

17 Cut two 7" (18 cm) pieces of 14g wire. Using the chasing hammer and steel bench block, hammer both pieces flat. Texture one side of each piece with the ball end of the chasing hammer (this will be the front). The wires have lengthened from the hammering and need to be recut to 7¼" (18.5 cm).

18 File the wire ends flat and using the round-nose pliers, create a simple loop on each wire facing the back (untextured side) of the wire. *note: This loop needs to be just big enough to slip the 16g wire through, and the tighter the fit, the better.*

assembling the bracelet

19 Slip one of the 14g wires onto the 1½" (3.8 cm) pin up against the 90º bend. With the looped arms of the clasp aligned with the outer loops on the woven strip, slip the clasp and woven section onto the pin, followed by the last 14g wire. Compress the loops of the 14g wire with flat-nose pliers so it secures the pin. This should make it difficult to move the pin when tugged (**Fig. 6**).

20 Grasp one side of the pin with flat-nose pliers, placing the pliers against the side of the 14g wire. Bend the end of the pin toward the back of the bracelet, forming a 90º angle and securing all the components. Repeat on the other end of the bracelet.

21 Fold the ends of each pin around the back of the bracelet (**Fig. 7**). Trim the pin wires so they are flush with the inside of the 14g wires (**Fig. 8**). Compress the bends in the pin wires with flat-nose pliers to secure. File the pin edges to create a smooth surface (**Fig. 9**).

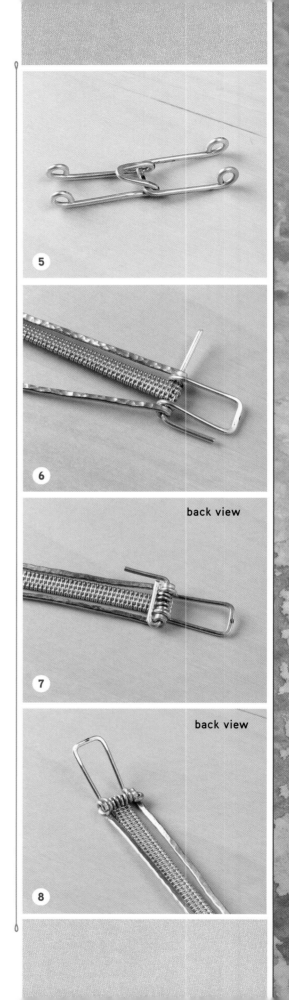

back view

back view

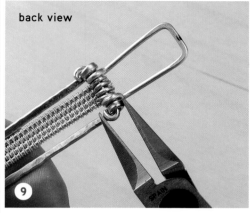
back view

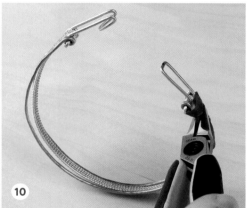

forming and finishing touches

22 Using the rawhide mallet and bracelet mandrel, begin forming the finished bracelet around the mandrel. *tip: Because the looped ends are on the back of the bracelet, it will not completely mold around the mandrel.*

23 Use your thumbs to gently curve the ends of the bracelet. If needed, use flat-nose pliers to help shape the tips **(Fig. 10)**.

24 When you are satisfied with the overall shape, put the bracelet back on the mandrel and hammer and reform with the rawhide mallet.

25 Oxidize the bracelet with liver of sulfur and polish with the steel wool and brass brush. Use a polishing cloth or a tumbler to clean and brighten the jewelry.

variations

Create a bracelet in copper (left). For a fun twist, make a silver version (right) that keeps the full length of the hammered 14g wires. Cross the wires over the woven strip when assembling. Lash the wires together with 26g wire where they cross. Secure the 26g wire to the bottom 14g wire before trimming.

MATERIALS

22¼" (56.5 cm) of 18g sterling silver wire

15' (4.6 m) of 28g fine silver wire

TOOLS

Ruler

Flush cutters or wire cutters

Tile

Protective eyewear

Cross-locking tweezers

Butane micro torch

Quenching bowl

Bobbin

Ring clamp (optional)

Rawhide mallet

Ring mandrel

Round-nose pliers

Liver of sulfur

#0000 extra-fine steel wool

Soft brass wire bristle brush or toothbrush

Polishing cloth (optional)

Rotary tumbler (optional)

embrace
ADJUSTABLE RING

The weave is beautiful on its own, but when combined with a splash of balled wire ends and a hint of a swirl, you get a wonderful, yet simple, adjustable ring.

level ⟹ **BEGINNER**

finished size ⟹ 7–10 (see Step 1 for more sizes)

RING SIZE	NUMBER OF WIRE PIECES	LENGTH
5–7	1	2½" (6.5 cm)
	6	3" (7.5 cm)
7–10	1	2¾" (7 cm)
	6	3¼" (8.5 cm)

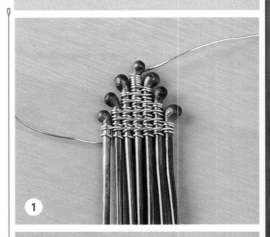

cutting the wire and balling the ends

1   Cut the amount of 18g wire needed for your ring size (see table above). *tip: Because the band is wide, I make the ring a size larger than what I usually wear.*

2   Place the tile on your work surface and put on the protective eyewear. Holding the wire with cross-locking tweezers, use the micro torch to ball up both ends of the wires, taking the time to make the balls small and as close to the same size as you can. Quench. Line up the finished wire from shortest to longest. *tip: When torching, you may end up with slightly different lengths. If you find that the ring is too small or too large, add or decrease the length by ⅛" (3 mm) the next time you make it. Alternatively, you can adjust how much you melt the ends. I tend to melt only ⅛" (3 mm) of wire on one end.*

3   Wind the 28g wire onto the bobbin.

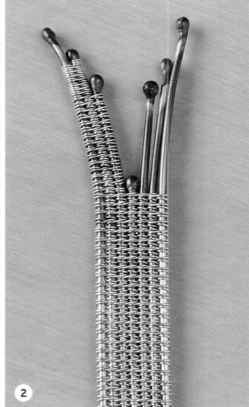

weaving

4   Using the ring clamp and starting with the shortest length of 18g wire, coil the 28g wire around one end just below the ball five times. Pick up the next two 18g wires in size and using the modified soumak weave, attach these new wires to the first so the balled ends sit just below the first ball on either side. Weave one more row after they have been attached.

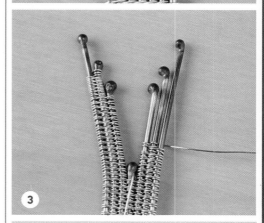

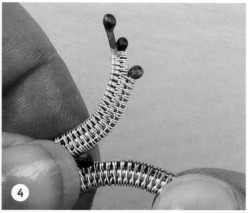

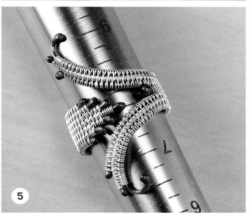

Fine silver wire is too soft to use for the whole ring. When I want to feature fine silver, I use sterling silver for the first and last base wires and fine silver for the rest of the base wires.

5 Pick up the next two 18g wires in size and place them on either side of the weave so the balls are just below the previous ones. Continue the modified soumak weave to attach the new wires to the base. Weave the five wires together for one more row. Add the last two 18g wires to either side of the weave as before, creating an arrow shape with the balled ends smoothly descending from the center point **(Fig. 1)**.

6 Continue weaving all seven base wires together until you reach the first balled end on the opposite end of the ring. Decrease the weave, only weaving with the first three wires on your left. Continue decreasing the weave as you reach each balled end. When you have one wire left, wrap the 28g wire around the balled end on the second wire twice, leaving the last wire exposed. Trim the excess 28g wire **(Fig. 2)**.

7 Use the remaining 28g wire to finish weaving the remaining three wires together as you did before. *tip: Wrap the 28g wire around the center wire first to help secure the 28g wire before continuing the weave.* End the weave on this side as you did in Step 6 **(Fig. 3)**.

forming

8 Using your fingers, spread the two woven arms apart and curve them into a gentle arc **(Fig. 4)**. Using the rawhide mallet, form the woven strip over the ring mandrel at the desired size. The two woven arms should embrace the arrow on either side as shown **(Fig. 5)**.

9 Using round-nose pliers, curl the two exposed ends outward.

finishing touches

10 Oxidize with liver of sulfur. Polish with the steel wool and brass brush. Use a polishing cloth or a tumbler to clean and brighten the jewelry.

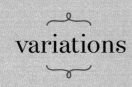

variations

Make a version of this ring in copper.

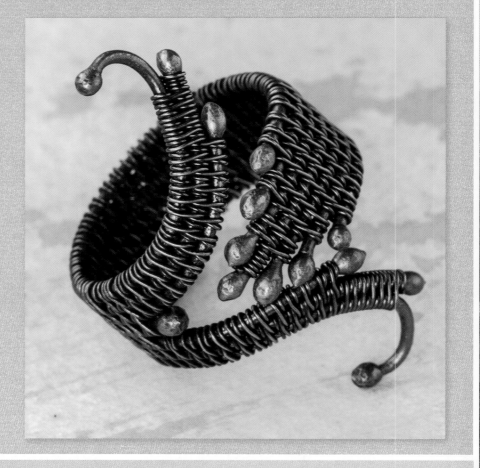

TECHNIQUES

Modified Soumak Weave (page 24)

Forming (page 21)

Balled Ends (page 33)

Coiling (page 35)

MATERIALS

24" (40.5 cm) of 18g fine silver wire

15' (3 m) of 28g fine silver wire

1 crystal heart briolette, 18x14mm

20" (50.8 cm) of sterling silver 1.5mm oval link chain with spring ring attached

TOOLS

Ruler

Flush cutters or wire cutters

Fine-point permanent marker

Round-nose pliers

Flat-nose pliers

Bobbin

Tile

Protective eyewear

Cross-locking tweezers

Butane micro torch

Quenching bowl

Ring clamp (optional)

Liver of sulfur

#0000 extra-fine steel wool

Soft brass wire bristle brush or toothbrush

Polishing cloth (optional)

Rotary tumbler (optional)

rivulet
PENDANT

I used to practice making woven strips and shaping them to see what would happen. This pendant plays on this idea; it's freeform, organic, and fun to twist and turn the weave.

level ⟹ **BEGINNER**

finished size ⟹ Pendant, ¾" wide x 2½" long (2 x 6.5 cm)

length ⟹ 20" (51 cm) long

cutting and forming the wire

1 Cut the 18g wire into two 12" (30.5 cm) pieces. Mark the center of each wire with the permanent marker.

2 Bend one 12" (30.5 cm) wire around the back of the round-nose pliers at the center mark, making a "U" shape. This will be Wire 1.

3 Using flat-nose pliers, fold the second 12" (30.5 cm) wire in half at the center mark. This will be Wire 2. Place Wire 2 inside Wire 1 and adjust the curves so Wire 2 nestles within Wire 1 and both wires are touching.

4 Wind the 28g wire onto a bobbin or work off the spool.

weaving

5 Mark Wire 1 at ¼" (6 mm) from the curve. Line up Wire 2 at the ¼" (6 mm) mark on Wire 1 **(Fig. 1)**. Hold both wires in place and trim the ends so they are graduated and come to a point.

6 Place the tile on your work surface and put on the protective eyewear. Holding the wire with cross-locking tweezers, use the micro torch to ball the ends of each wire. Quench **(Fig. 2)**. *tip: If you don't have a torch, create a paddle on the very tips of the wire and round the edges with a file.*

7 Place Wire 2 back inside Wire 1. Leaving a 2" (5 cm) tail, use the 28g wire to weave Wires 1 and 2 together at the ¼" (6 mm) mark using the modified soumak weave. Weave for one row **(Fig. 3)**.

8 Using your fingers, pull Wire 2 down toward the weave, creating a space between the shaped ends. This will become the bail **(Fig. 4)**.

9 Continue weaving Wires 1 and 2 together until you reach the first balled end. *tip: If your hands become fatigued, use the ring clamp to hold Wires 1 and 2 together.* At the first balled end, decrease the weave.

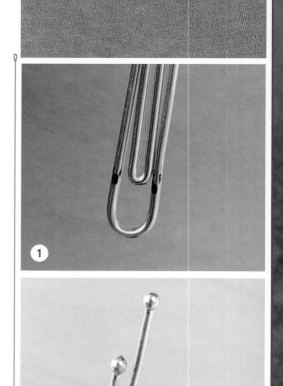

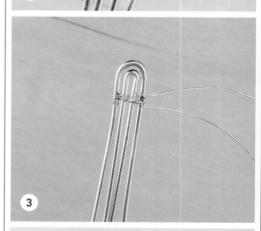

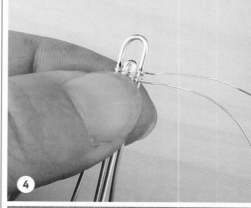

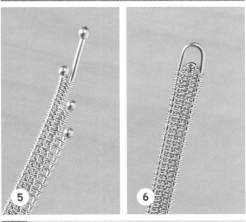

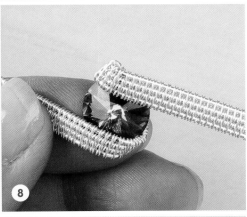
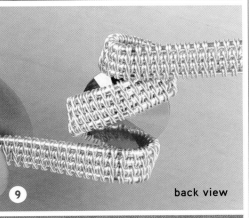

back view

10 Continue to decrease the weave at each ball. When you reach the third balled end, leave enough space to wrap twice around the wire below the third ball. Trim the 28g wire **(Fig. 5)**.

11 Coil the remaining 28g tail at the opposite end around Wire 2 and trim **(Fig. 6)**.

forming

12 Mark the center of the woven strip with the permanent marker. Place the crystal just above the center mark. With your fingers, mold the woven strip to the back of the crystal **(Fig. 7)**. *tip: If you don't have a crystal, choose any 15mm–18mm cabochon or faceted stone for the center. This necklace also looks great without a center stone.*

13 Bend the bottom and lower portions of the woven strip over the front of the crystal **(Fig. 8)**. *tip: Don't be afraid to use force to shape the weave. Your fingers will not damage the strip, and you want exaggerated bends.*

14 Adjust the angle of the arms so they cover the top and bottom edges of the crystal. Compress the strip to the crystal to create a snug fit.

15 Using your fingers, fold the two arms back around the crystal in an organic spiral **(Fig. 9)**.

16 Check the back of the woven strip to make sure it covers the back edges of the crystal; this will secure the crystal inside the shaped strip. If the crystal is loose, adjust the shape or angle of the woven arms.

If you need to use pliers, cover the woven strip with painter's tape to protect it.

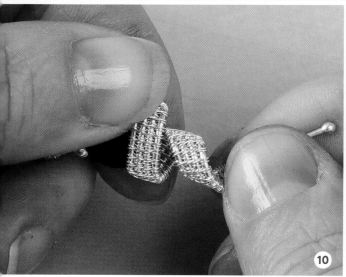

17 Continue to shape the two woven arms with your fingers, folding or twisting the strip in an alternating pattern to form a loose spiral (**Fig. 10**). As you shape the top half, pivot the woven strip away from you so it's perpendicular to the crystal. The opening of the bail should be visible (**Fig. 11**).

finishing touches

18 Using round-nose pliers, shape the bail so it follows the serpentine shape (**Fig. 12**). Readjust or compress the bends in the weave with your fingers or pliers as needed until you are pleased with the finished design (**Fig. 13**).

19 Oxidize the pendant and chain in liver of sulfur and polish with the steel wool and brass brush. Use a polishing cloth or a tumbler to clean and brighten the jewelry.

variations

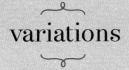

Use an oval green crystal with fine silver wire to make the variation pictured here. You could also use copper wire and skip the center stone. Use two 8" (15 cm) pieces of 18g wire to make a shorter pendant. For stones 12mm–15mm, cut two 10" (25.4 cm) lengths; use longer lengths to capture larger stones. For larger stones, you can also increase the gauge to 16g. A heavier, wider woven strip will help balance the design.

TECHNIQUES

Modified Soumak Weave (page 24)

Decreasing the Weave (page 24)

Coiling (page 35)

Balled Ends (page 33)

Hammering (page 32)

Filing (page 33)

MATERIALS

12" (30.5 cm) of 18g fine silver wire

6' (183 cm) of 28g fine silver wire

TOOLS

Ruler

Flush cutters or wire cutters

Steel ring-sizing mandrel

Flat-nose pliers

Tile

Metal pan of water

Protective eyewear

Cross-locking tweezers

Butane micro torch

Chasing hammer

Square needle file

Painter's tape

Rawhide mallet

Liver of sulfur

#0000 extra-fine steel wool

Soft brass wire bristle brush of toothbrush

Polishing cloth (optional)

Tumbler (optional)

orbit
RING

The rough nuggets set this ring apart. My inspiration came from coupling the faceted chunks of metal in rings and pendants with weaving.

level ⇒ **BEGINNER**

finished size ⇒ 5–9, ¼" (6 mm) wide
(see Step 1 for more sizes)

cutting and forming the wires

1 Cut three 4" (10 cm) pieces of 18g wire. *note: For a ring size larger than a size 9, cut three 5" (12.5 cm) pieces of 18g wire and 7' (2.1 m) of 28g wire.*

2 Shape one 4" (10 cm) wire around the ring mandrel at half a size larger than your desired finished ring size. Grasp the ends of the wire with flat-nose pliers and twist them together, creating a tight twist.

3 Trim the twisted wire to ⅜" (1 cm), or smaller for a smaller nugget **(Fig. 1)**.

4 Place the tile on your work surface with the pan of water on top. Put on the protective eyewear. Holding the wire with cross-locking tweezers, use the micro torch to melt the full length of the twisted wires until a large ball forms that is flush with the ring shank. *tip: If you're having trouble melting the wire, pivot the wire tip straight into the flame. Once it starts to melt, slowly rotate your wrist to bring the wire back up to the perpendicular position.*

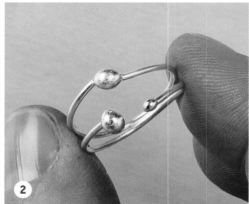

5 Repeat Steps 2–4 with the remaining two wires, creating a total of three rings **(Fig. 2)**. *note: If you melt past the ring, severing the enclosed connection, the ring is still usable. There is no need to discard and start anew. Simply melt the severed tip to form a tiny little ball. This will give you a large nugget on one end and a small one on the other and can be incorporated into your ring. This can be seen in the variations on page 79.*

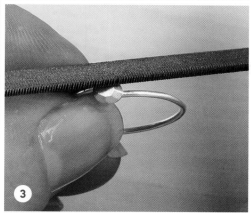

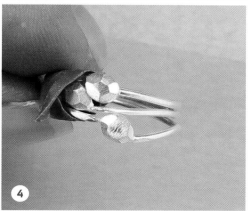

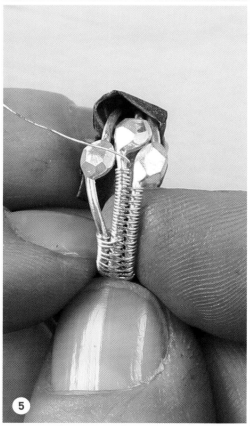

creating the faceted nuggets

6 Slide one ring onto the ring mandrel and using the chasing hammer, slightly flatten the top of the melted ball. Repeat with the remaining rings.

7 Using the square needle file, create angled planes along the sides of the flattened nugget to give it a rough, faceted shape **(Fig. 3)**.

weaving

8 Stack the rings together so the nuggets line up and fit together in a pleasing way. Tape one half of the ring together, from the center and up one side, ensuring each individual ring stays in place as you weave **(Fig. 4)**.

9 Starting in the center of the rings, thread 36" (91.5 cm) of the 28g wire between Rings 1 and 2.

10 Weave all three rings together using the modified soumak weave, weaving up toward the nuggets, threading the 28g wire through the opening between the nuggets as you weave. *note: The ring will end up misshapen, but will be reshaped after weaving in Step 14.*

11 As you weave closer to the top, one of the outer rings will start to veer away from the other two. At this point, decrease the weave and weave only the other two rings together until you reach the middle nugget as shown. Decrease the weave, coiling only around the third ring until you reach the nugget. Trim the 28g wire flush **(Fig. 5)**.

12 Remove the tape and weave the second half of the ring.

Weaving in an enclosed space is more difficult because you can't simply wrap around the base wires. Instead, you will be threading the 28g wires between the base wires, which work-hardens the 28g wire much more quickly, therefore causing it to potentially break with more frequency. I recommend that your first ring use only three base wires, as shown in this project. Challenge yourself by adding more base wires for a second ring, if you like, creating a thicker band.

finishing touches

13 Use the leftover 28g wire to coil any exposed ring wires. Trim the excess 28g wire flush on the inside of the ring **(Fig. 6)**.

14 Use the rawhide hammer to gently shape the finished ring around the ring mandrel at your desired size.

15 Oxidize the ring with liver of sulfur and polish with the steel wool and brass brush. Use a polishing cloth or a tumbler to clean and polish the jewelry.

The 28g wire can be secured either by coiling it around a base wire or by puncturing the weave one row down with a beading awl and securing it the same way you would in the Woven Stacking Bracelet (page 56).

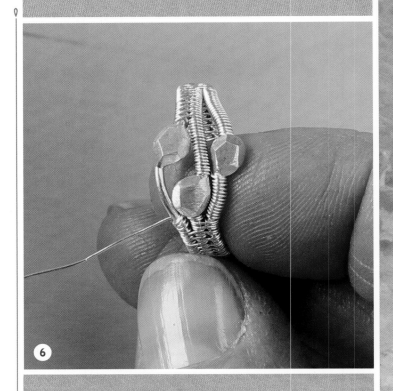

6

variations

Make this ring with four base wires (right) or five base wires (left). Instead of faceting the nuggets, hammer them flat to create paved stones instead. If making this ring in copper, it is easier to use a propane torch because it has a larger, hotter flame than a micro torch. This not only makes the process quicker, but it also means that you can hold the copper anywhere in the flame, not just in one spot. Remember to still keep the pan of water below the flame.

TECHNIQUES

Modified Soumak Weave (page 24)

Balled Ends (page 33)

Forming (page 21)

Lashing Weave (page 26)

Hammering (page 32)

Filing (page 33)

Embellishing (page 35)

Annealing (page 20)

Symmetry (page 34)

MATERIALS

7.5" (19 cm) of 14g fine silver wire

52½" (133.5 cm) of 18g fine silver wire

35" (89 cm) of 26g fine silver wire

30' (9.1 m) of 28g fine silver wire on a bobbin

1" (2.5 cm) of sterling silver 3mm cable chain (optional)

7 sterling silver rounds, 2mm

14 round green freshwater pearls, 5mm

1 sterling silver jump ring, 4mm

1 sterling silver lobster-claw clasp, 11mm

TOOLS

Ruler

Flush cutters or wire cutters

Tile

Protective eyewear

Cross-locking tweezers

Butane micro torch

Quenching bowl

Chasing hammer

Steel bench block

Fine-point permanent marker

Metal hole punch, 1.25mm

Needle file

Charcoal block or fire brick

Round-nose pliers

Chain-nose pliers

5mm dowel

Flat-nose pliers

Stainless steel ring-sizing mandrel

Liver of sulfur

#0000 extra-fine steel wool

Brass wire bristle brush or toothbrush

Polishing cloth (optional)

Tumbler (optional)

petal
BRACELET

Small and simple, the petal-shaped component featured in this bracelet is very versatile. Add it to a chain, make a pair into earrings, string one on a necklace as a simple pendant, or add a lobster claw to one link to make a decorative clasp.

level ⇒ **INTERMEDIATE**

length ⇒ 7¼" (18.5 cm)

preparing the wire

1 Cut six 1" (2.5 cm) pieces of 14g wire and one 1½" (3.8 cm) piece of 14g wire. Put the tile on your work surface and put on the protective eyewear. Holding the wire with cross-locking tweezers, use the micro torch to ball up one end of each wire (see page 33). Quench. Using the chasing hammer and steel bench block, hammer a paddle on the other end of each wire that is 3 mm in width. For the 1½" (3.8 cm) piece, be sure to paddle ½" (1.3 cm) of the end. Mark the center of each paddle on the 1" (2.5 cm) lengths at the top with the permanent marker. Punch a 1.25 mm hole at the mark with the hole punch. Round the edges of each paddle with the file. Place the charcoal block on your work surface and anneal your 1½" (3.8 cm) length. With the round-nose pliers, roll the paddle into a loop until the 1½" (3.8 cm) length is the same size as the 1" (2.5 cm) lengths and the paddled loop is rolled onto itself. Mark the centers of all the 14g lengths **(Fig. 1)**.

2 Cut fourteen 2¼" (5.5 cm) pieces of 18g wire. Ball up one end on each wire with the micro torch.

3 Cut seven 3" (7.5 cm) pieces of 18g wire. Mark the centers. Using chain-nose pliers, bend each wire to a 90° angle at the mark.

weaving

4 Position the balled end of each 2¼" (5.5 cm) 18g wire on either side of the paddled end of the 1" (2.5 cm) 14g wire as shown. The hole in the paddle should be perpendicular to the balled ends, and the balled ends should be below the hole in the paddle. The wires will be referred to from left to right: Wire 1, 2, and 3.

5 Pull out 12" (30.5 cm) of your 28g wire and begin the weave in the middle of the 14g wire with your 12" (30.5 cm) length, making sure you keep the rest of your 28g wire on your bobbin. Weave all three wires together using the modified soumak weave, using the 12" (30.5 cm) to weave with, and weaving toward the balled-up 18g ends. *note: Because we are working with such a short length, I find it easier to work from the center out so that we have something for our fingers to grip onto as we weave.* When you reach the balled ends, flip the woven form and weave the other half, stopping at the balled end on the 14g wire **(Fig. 2)**.

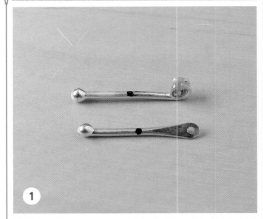

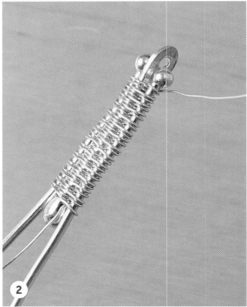

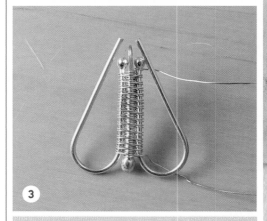

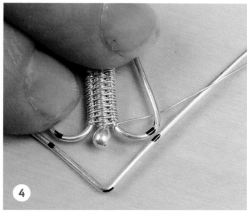

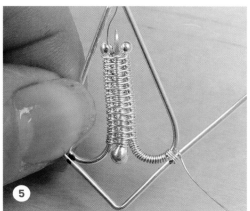

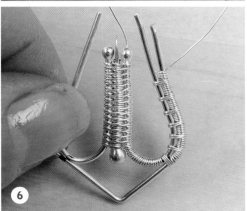

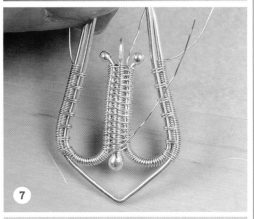

6 Bend Wires 1 and 3 around the 5mm dowel, forming two "U" shapes that are mirror images **(Fig. 3)**. Center one V-shaped wire from Step 3 below the balled end of the 14g wire, so the two arms of the "V" touch the bottom of the "U" shapes. This is Wire 4. Use the permanent marker to mark all the wires where they touch **(Fig. 4)**.

7 Coil the 28g wire around the curve of Wire 3 until you reach the mark on the right arm of Wire 3. Make sure the marks are lined up properly and that the "V" still looks centered. Lash Wires 3 and 4 together three times **(Fig. 5)**. Using your fingers, bend the right arm of Wire 4 so it follows the curve of the right arm of Wire 3.

8 Coil around the right arm of Wire 4 six times. Lash Wires 3 and 4 together twice. Continue this pattern (coiling Wire 4 six times and lashing Wires 3 and 4 together twice) until you have a total of six sets of coils and lashes. End by coiling around Wire 4 three times, finishing with the wire on the back. Cut the 28g wire, leaving a 2" (5 cm) tail **(Fig. 6)**.

9 Add a new 28g wire to the curve of Wire 1 where it comes out of the weave, leaving enough of a tail to grip with as you begin your coils. Coil around Wire 1 until you reach the mark on the arm of Wire 1. *note: If you would like, you can slip a 3mm chain onto the "V" wire, Wire 4, at this time to add an extension to the bracelet; this will also be where you will slip Wire 4 through the hole in Wire 2 of the previous link to connect the bracelet together.* Make sure the two marks line up before lashing Wires 1 and 4 together three times. Bend Wire 4 so it follows the curve of Wire 1 as shown.

10 Coil Wire 4 six times and then lash Wires 4 and 1 together twice. Continue this coiling and lashing pattern (as you did in Step 8) until you have six sets. End by coiling around Wire 4 three times. Cut the 28g wire on the back, leaving a 2" (5 cm) tail **(Fig. 7)**.

forming

11 Using chain-nose pliers, bend the balled ends on Wires 1 and 3 away from Wire 2 **(Fig. 8)**.

12 Reposition the dowel in the curve of Wire 3. Using your fingers, bend woven Wires 3 and 4 over the front of Wire 2, ending with Wire 4 just above the balled end of Wire 3. Using chain-nose pliers, grasp the tip of the right arm of Wire 4 and bend it back around the base of the balled end of Wire 3; do not complete the loop **(Fig. 9)**. Bend the tip of Wire 3 to the back as shown **(Fig. 10)**.

13 Repeat Step 12 with the left arm of Wire 4 and Wire 1, creating a mirror image of the other side.

14 String a 2mm round onto one of the 28g wires. Thread the other 28g tail through the opposite side of the round so the 28g wires crisscross inside the middle of the bead and in front of the woven form. Pull the 28g wires until the round is nestled between the two coiled arms at the top **(Fig. 11)**. Bring the 28g tails behind the coiled arms to the back of the weave. Secure the 28g tails by coiling twice around the base of the balled end on Wires 1 and 3. Trim all the tails flush.

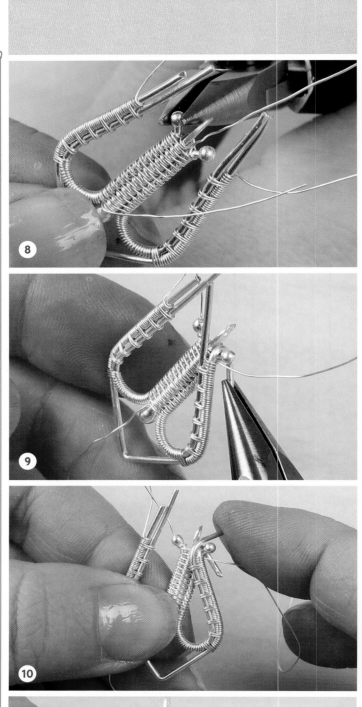

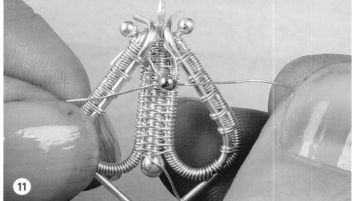

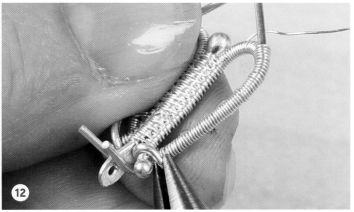

12

13

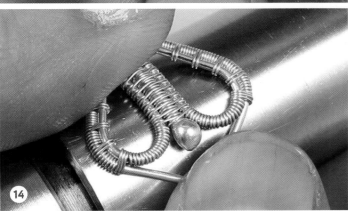

14

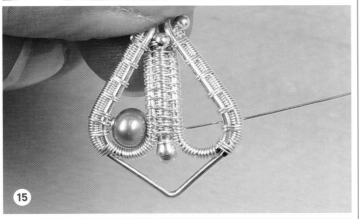

15

15 Using chain-nose pliers, wrap Wire 4 completely around the base of the balled ends on both sides **(Fig. 12)**. Trim the excess 18g wires of Wire 4. Trim Wires 1 and 3 just above the metal bead in the front **(Fig. 13)**.

16 Place the woven form right-side up at the size 16 mark on the ring mandrel. Use your fingers to gently curve the woven form over the mandrel **(Fig. 14)**.

final embellishments

17 Cut a 5" (12.5 cm) length of 26g wire. Wrap the center of the 26g wire around the balled end of the 14g wire, ending with the 26g wire tails on the back. *note: Steps 18 and 19 can be done after you have oxidized and polished the bracelet with some pre-oxidized 26g wire if you have concerns about dipping the pearls in the liver of sulfur.*

18 Thread one 26g tail wire through the curved loop on one side of the woven form. String one pearl onto the wire and center it in the curved section. Wrap the 26g wire around the outside of the two woven 18g wires and back up around to wrap twice around the wire passing through the pearl. Repeat on the other side. Trim the excess 26g wire **(Fig. 15)**.

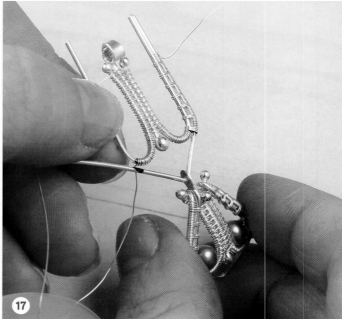

19 Repeat Steps 4–18 to create a total of six petal components. When you get to Step 9, slip the "V" wire onto the previous petal to link the bracelet together **(Fig. 16)**. The seventh link will be your 1½" (3.8 cm) length of 14g wire. After attaching this link, use a jump ring to attach the lobster claw to the loop you made with the 14g wire **(Fig. 17)**.

20 Oxidize the bracelet in liver of sulfur and polish with the steel wool and brass wire bristle brush. Use a polishing cloth or a tumbler to clean and polish the jewelry.

variation

Turn the petal component into stunning earrings by using 20g wire for the outside V-shaped wire, instead of 18g wire. Add 2mm silver rounds and long lengths of graduated chain to the V-shaped wire before lashing it to the woven form. Create balled-end head pins with 24g wire and flatten the balls with the hammer. Attach these head pins to the ends of the chain with wrapped loops. Follow the instructions on page 41 to create the French ear wires.

MATERIALS

1" (2.5 cm) of 14g fine silver wire

4" (10 cm) of 16g fine silver wire

7" (18 cm) of 18g fine silver wire

1' (30.5 cm) of 22g fine silver wire

5' (152.5 cm) of 28g fine silver wire

2 sterling silver rounds, 2mm

3 sterling silver rounds, 3mm

5 crystal bicones, 4mm

1 crystal pendant drop, 11mm

18½" (47 cm) of sterling silver 2mm flat oval chain

Simple S-clasp (see page 43 for materials and instructions)

TOOLS

Ruler

Flush cutters or wire cutters

Needle files

Fine-point permanent marker

Chasing hammer

Steel bench block

Metal hole punch, 1.25mm

Painter's tape

Round-nose pliers

Chain-nose pliers

Dowels ranging in sizes from 2–6mm (optional)

Liver of sulfur

#0000 extra-fine steel wool

Soft brass wire bristle brush or toothbrush

Soft polishing cloth (optional)

Tumbler (optional)

florence
PENDANT

Simple and sweet, the Florence pendant is a great introduction to creating symmetrical wirework.

level ⇒ **INTERMEDIATE**

finished size ⇒ 1⅛" wide x 1⅛" high (2.8 x 2.8 cm)

length ⇒ 18½" (47 cm)

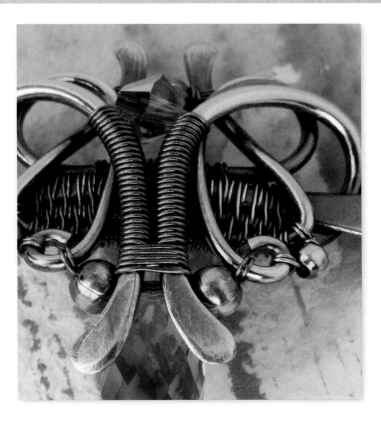

cutting and forming the wires

1 Cut 1" (2.5 cm) of 14g wire and file the ends flat. Mark the center of each wire with the permanent marker. Using the chasing hammer and steel bench block, create a paddle on each end that is 3–3.5 mm wide. Mark the center of the paddled ends and then punch holes at the marks with the hole punch. Round the paddled ends with the file and remove any burrs made while punching the holes.

2 Cut 4" (10 cm) of 16g wire, 4" (10 cm) of 18g wire, and 3" (7.5 cm) of 18g wire. Mark the center of each wire.

weaving

3 Line the wires up at the center marks starting with the 4" (10 cm) 18g wire, followed by the 14g wire, the 16g wire, and the 3" (7.5 cm) 18g wire. Using your fingers, curve the 16g and 18g wires so they are flush against the paddled 14g wire. Tape the wires together at the center marks. The wires will now be referenced by number: the 4" (10 cm) 18g wire (on the left) will be Wire 1, followed by Wires 2, 3, and 4.

4 Cut 3' (91.5 cm) of 28g wire. Starting in the center of the 28g wire, weave all four wires together using the modified soumak weave. Weave three complete rows.

5 Decrease the weave, weaving Wires 2, 3, and 4 together for another four rows. Stop the weave around Wire 4, with the 28g wire in the back **(Fig. 1)**.

6 Remove the tape and flip the woven form over. Weave all four wires together for another three rows. Decrease the weave, weaving Wires 3 and 4 together for four rows, ending the weave around Wire 4, with the 28g wire in the back.

7 Re-mark the center of the weave with the permanent marker as shown **(Fig. 2)**. *tip: Sometimes the base wires shift while weaving, so I use the weave to gauge where the center is and draw a line down the center row.*

Use the center line as a reference point to ensure accurately shaped, symmetrical wires from side to side.

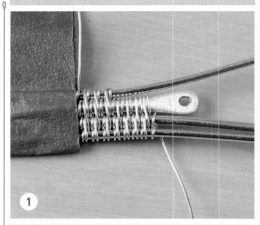

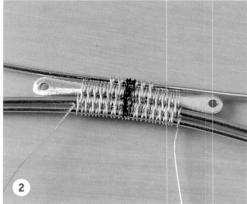

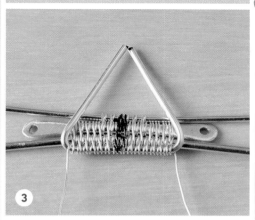

3

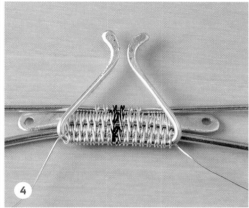

4

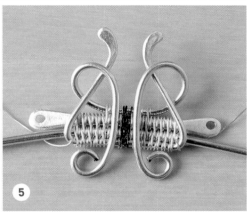

5

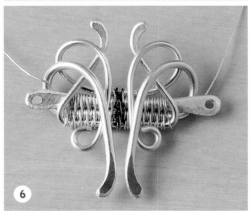

6

forming

8 Trim Wire 1 at 1½" (3.8 cm) from the end of the weave before it decreased. Trim Wire 3 at 1⅜" (3.5 cm) from the end of the weave. Trim Wire 4 at ¾" (2 cm) from the end of the weave. File the ends flat.

9 Bend Wire 4 up over the weave to form a triangle with the ends touching **(Fig. 3)**. Curve the ends of Wire 4 outward using round-nose pliers. Place the form on the edge of the steel bench block as shown and create a paddle on each end of Wire 4 with the chasing hammer. Round the paddled ends with the file **(Fig. 4)**.

10 Using your fingers, bend the left side of Wire 1 up and around, forming a loop, crossing over Wire 4, and then straight down over the weave to the left of the center mark. Repeat, creating a mirror loop with the right side of Wire 1. *tip: If the flat ends of Wire 1 are uneven at the bottom, then the loops are not symmetrical. Using round-nose pliers or dowels, adjust the loops until the ends line up.* Use the tip of the round-nose pliers to create a simple loop on the ends of Wire 1 with the loops facing outward and against the bottom edge of the weave **(Fig. 5)**.

11 Bend the left side of Wire 3 up and behind Wire 2, form a loop (making sure not to block the Wire 2 holes), and then bend Wire 3 straight down over the weave. Create a mirror loop on the right side of Wire 3. Adjust the loops as needed so the flat ends are even. Use the tip of the round-nose pliers to curve the ends of Wire 3 outward. Create a paddle on the ends of Wire 3, as you did in Step 9, making sure that only the Wire 3 ends are on the steel bench block. This will prevent accidently hammering the loops. Round the paddled ends with the file **(Fig. 6)**.

If the ends do not line up evenly, then the shaping is uneven. If it looks even and symmetrical in the front, check the back. A lot of shaping mistakes happen in the back where you can't see them.

adding embellishments

12 String one 2mm round onto the 28g wire. Bring the 28g wire over to Wire 1 (on the right) and wrap twice around the loop. Thread the 28g wire back through the 2mm round. Wrap once around Wire 4 before securing the 28g wire by wrapping twice around the wire holding the 2mm round. Repeat on the other side. Trim the excess 28g wire **(Fig. 7)**.

13 Cut 6" (15 cm) of 28g wire. String one 3mm round onto the center of the wire. Center the 3mm round between the curved ends of Wire 4 as shown and coil the 28g wire around each side of Wire 4 twice before going back through the 3mm round. Wrap the 28g wire one more time around Wire 4. Secure the 28g wire as in Step 12. Trim the excess 28g wire **(Fig. 8)**.

14 Cut 18" (45.5 cm) of 28g wire. String one crystal bicone onto the center of the wire. Thread the 28g wire behind the "arms" of Wire 3 so the crystal bicone sits between them. Coil the 28g wire down the arms of Wire 3 as shown, stopping just before the wire ends curve out **(Fig. 9)**. Use one 28g wire to lash the ends of Wire 3 together twice **(Fig. 10)**.

15 Thread the crystal pendant drop onto the 28g wire and continue to lash around the ends of Wire 3 twice, making sure to pass through the hole of the pendant as you make the final lashings **(Fig. 11)**. *tip: If the pendant hole is too small for the 28g wire to pass through more than once, go across the back of the pendant as you lash around Wire 3.*

16 Thread the other 28g wire through the pendant so it is coming out the opposite end of the first 28g wire **(Fig. 12)**. If the 28g wire won't fit through the hole, thread it through the lashings on the back. String one 3mm round onto the 28g wire and cross over to the loop on Wire 1 (on the right). Wrap twice around the loop before threading the 28g wire back through the 3mm round. Repeat on the other side **(Fig. 13)**.

17 To secure the 28g wires, cross them over the pendant in the back and wrap twice around the wire holding the 3mm rounds in place beside the pendant. Trim the excess 28g wire.

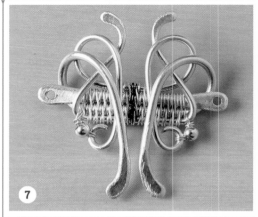

7

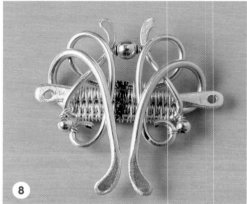

8

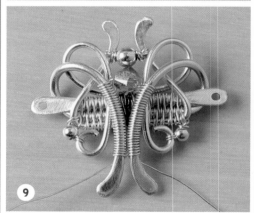

9

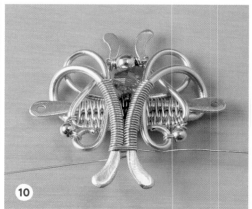

10

11

back view

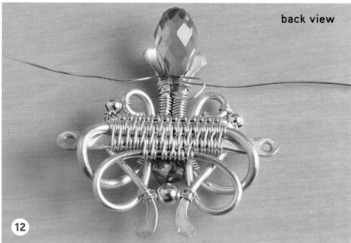

12

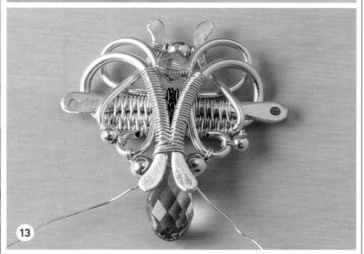

13

finishing touches

18 Cut the 22g wire into four 3" (7.5 cm) lengths. Create three crystal bicone links by stringing one 4mm crystal bicone onto each wire and begin a wrapped loop on each end; do not wrap the loops. Thread one loop of one link through the left hole in Wire 2 and complete the wrap on that loop. Repeat, attaching a second link to the right hole of Wire 2 and complete the wrap on that loop. Attach one end of each length of chain to the free loops on the first and second link; complete the wraps. Attach one loop of the third link to the free end of one chain and attach the other loop to the S-clasp; complete the wraps. Create a final link with one loop big enough to fit the hook of the S-clasp through; complete the wrap on that loop. Attach the second loop to the remaining free end of the chain; complete the wrap.

19 Oxidize the complete necklace with liver of sulfur and polish with the steel wool and brass brush. Use a polishing cloth or a tumbler to clean and brighten the jewelry.

At first glance, symmetry seems easy, but being off by ¹⁄₁₆" (2 mm) can skew the design and cause the ends to not line up properly.

TECHNIQUES

Modified Soumak Weave (page 24)

Balled Ends (page 33)

Forming (page 21)

Loops (page 27)

Lashing (page 18)

Hammering (page 32)

MATERIALS

3½" (9 cm) of 18g fine silver wire

10" (25.5 cm) of 20g fine silver wire

5' (152.5 cm) of 28g fine silver wire

2 lavender pearls, 6mm

2 sterling silver ear nuts with a hole size of .032" (0.8 mm)

TOOLS

Ruler

Flush cutters or wire cutters

Fine-point permanent marker

Round-nose pliers

Chasing hammer

Steel bench block

Flat-nose pliers

Tile

Protective eyewear

Butane micro torch

Cross-locking tweezers

Quenching bowl

5.5mm dowel

Needle file

Liver of sulfur

#0000 extra-fine steel wool

Soft brass wire bristle brush or toothbrush

Polishing cloth (optional)

Tumbler (optional)

danika
POST EARRINGS

These earrings were inspired by my mother, who challenged me to design a pair of post earrings that were dainty, simple, and versatile.

level ⇒ **INTERMEDIATE**

finished length ⇒ ⅜" wide x ⅞" long (1 x 2.2 cm)

cutting the wire and balling the ends

1 Cut two 1¾" (4.5 cm) pieces of 18g wire. Use the permanent marker to make a line on both jaws of the round-nose pliers, just below the tip. This mark will serve as a guide to ensure that the loops are the same size. Grasp the end of one wire with the round-nose pliers, at the mark, and make a simple loop. Repeat on the other end of the wire, making sure the loops are going in the same direction. Repeat, creating matching loops on the second piece of wire. Using the chasing hammer and steel bench block, flare out the loop (see page 32) on one end of each wire. Mark the wires ½" (1.3 cm) and 1" (2.5 cm) from the tip of the loop that was not hammered.

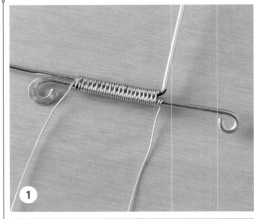

2 Cut two 4" (10 cm) pieces of 20g wire. Mark each wire ¾" (2 cm) in on one end. Using flat-nose pliers, bend each wire at the mark into a right angle, forming an "L" shape. Cut two 2" (5 cm) pieces of 20g wire. Place the tile on your work surface and put on the protective eyewear. Ball up both ends of each wire with the torch, holding the wire with crosslocking tweezers, so the finished length of each is 1½" (3.8 cm). Quench. Mark the center of each balled end wire, ¾" (2 cm) in from the tip of a balled end.

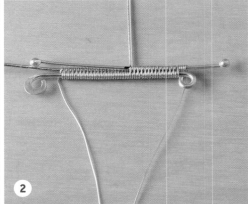

3 Cut two 2½' (76 cm) pieces of 28g wire.

weaving

4 Place one 4" (10 cm) piece of 20g wire over one 18g wire. The loops on the 18g wire should be facing down, with the hammered loop on the left. The longer section of the 20g wire should be on the left, with the shorter section facing up, and the bend should line up with the ½" (1.3 cm) mark on the 18g wire.

5 Leaving a 6" (15 cm) tail and starting at the 1" (2.5 cm) mark on the 18g wire, use one 2½' (76 cm) piece of 28g wire to weave the two base wires together with the modified soumak weave **(Fig. 1)**.

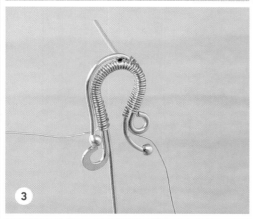

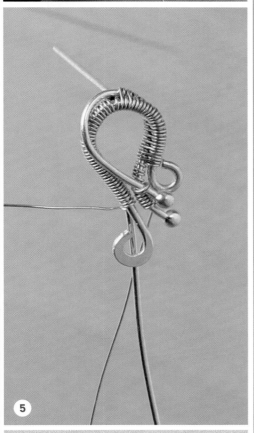

6 Stop the weave when you reach the ½" (1.3 cm) mark on the 18g wire. Coil the 28g wire around the 18g wire twice. Take one 20g wire with balled ends and line up the center mark to the ½" (1.3 cm) mark on the 18g wire, with the 20g wire on top of the "L." Weave the balled end wire to the 18g wire until you reach the loop on the end of the 18g wire. Coil the 28g wire around the balled end wire four times. Set the woven form aside **(Fig. 2)**.

7 Repeat Steps 4–6 to weave the remaining 4" (10 cm) 20g and 18g base wires together for the second earring. After weaving these base wires together, flip the woven form over to create a mirror image of the first woven form. Weave the remaining balled end wire to the 18g wire as in Steps 5–6 and finish by coiling the 28g wire around the balled end wire four times.

forming

8 Pick up the woven form set aside in Step 6. Line up the short section of the 20g wire with the center of the 5.5mm dowel, making sure the loop that was not hammered is on the right and facing down. Bend the woven section around the dowel, keeping the short section of the 20g wire as centered as possible on the dowel, forming a teardrop shape.

9 Hold the woven form so the 18g wire is in front. Using flat-nose pliers, grasp the 18g loops and rotate them outward and away from the center **(Fig. 3)**. Curve the balled end wire on the bottom right slightly around the 18g loop.

10 Place the woven form back on the 5.5mm dowel and bring the ends closer together **(Fig. 4)**. Using round-nose pliers, curve the top balled end wire down and over the woven form toward the bottom. Take the 28g wire that is coiled around the opposite end of the balled end wire and lash it twice around both the balled end wires, just above the front balled end. Continue coiling down the balled end wire in the back five more times **(Fig. 5)**.

11 Flip the woven form over to the back and trim the longer section of 20g wire to 2" (5 cm) from the end of the weave. Flip the woven form to the front and use the tip of the round-nose pliers to make a simple loop at the end, facing the same direction as the hammered 18g loop.

12 Position the back of the round-nose pliers (or a 4mm dowel) between the hammered loop on the left and the back balled end wire. Wrap the 20g wire around the pliers and along the outside of the front balled end wire on the right (**Fig. 6**). Lash the back balled end wire to the curved 20g wire twice. Finish coiling down the back balled end wire toward the ball and trim the 28g wire flush (**Fig. 7**).

13 Using round-nose pliers, grasp the loop on the 20g wire and swirl the wire inward. Position the swirl over the top of the woven form (**Fig. 8**).

Because you will be working in such a small area, it's important that your measurements are as exact as possible. Being even ¹⁄₁₆" (2 mm) off can alter the design and may make it difficult to line up the wires properly when shaping.

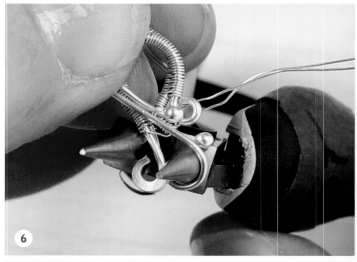

6

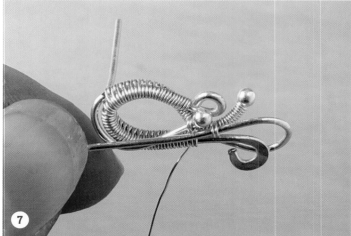

7

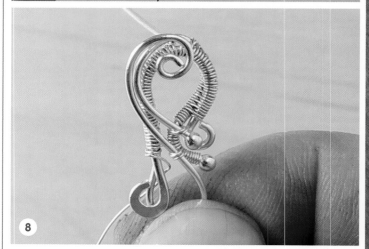

8

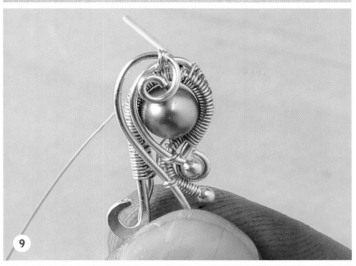

Fig. 9

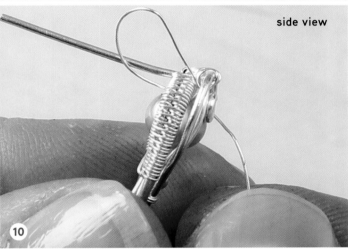

side view

Fig. 10

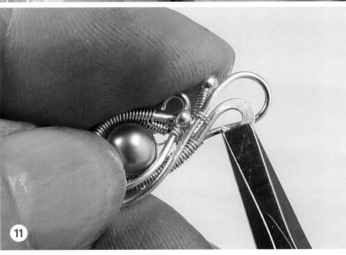

Fig. 11

final touches

14 Bring the remaining 28g wire to the back of the woven form and string one pearl onto the wire. Thread the 28g wire through the two 20g wires at the top of the earring. Lash the two wires together three times. *tip: Steps 14–19 can be done after you have oxidized the earrings if you have concerns about placing the pearls in liver of sulfur* (**Fig. 9**).

15 Bring the 28g wire to the back of the weave and wrap around the weave so that the 28g wire is in the front (**Fig. 10**). Lift the 20g loop up with your fingernail. Push the pearl forward with your fingers to expose the hole. Pass the 28g wire back through the pearl. *tip: If you can't thread the 28g wire back through the pearl for a second time, then secure the 28g wire around the wire passing through the pearl. Be careful not to pull too hard on the wire; it's easy to break it as you tighten. If you do break the wire, trim the broken 28g wire. Add a new one to attach the pearl by wrapping the weaving wire around a base wire three times before finishing Steps 14–15.*

16 Wrap the 28g wire once around the 20g wire in the back and then wrap it twice around the 28g wires holding the pearl in place. Trim the 28g wire flush.

17 Push the 20g loop back down on top of the pearl. Using flat-nose pliers, grasp the hammered loop and push it in so it sits off center inside the large 20g wire loop (**Fig. 11**).

18 Trim the straight 20g wire on the back of the earring to ⅜" (1 cm), forming the post. Round the cut edges of the post with the file. Add the ear nut to the post.

19 Repeat Steps 8–18 to complete the second earring, making sure to form the wires so the second earring is a mirror image of the first. *tip: The easiest way to create a mirror image is to flip the woven strip over after weaving the "L" wire and just before you begin inserting the balled wire into the weave.*

20 Oxidize the earrings in liver of sulfur. Polish with the steel wool and brass brush. Use a polishing cloth or a tumbler to clean and brighten the jewelry.

variation

To make dangle earrings, use silver wire and pink AB crystals to create two wire-wrapped links and attach them to the bottom loop of each earring. Or use ball-end head pins and pink AB crystals to create seven wrapped-loop dangles. Attach two dangles on either side of the top wrapped link. Attach two dangles on either side of the middle wrapped link. Attach one dangle to the bottom loop of the last wrapped link.

TECHNIQUES

Modified Soumak Weave (page 24)

Balled Ends (page 33)

Loops (page 27)

Lashing (page 18)

Forming (page 21)

Hammering (page 32)

Embellishing (page 35)

Puncturing the Weave (page 18)

MATERIALS

4" (10 cm) of 16g copper wire

6" (15 cm) of 18g copper wire

9" (23 cm) of 22g copper wire

12" (30.5 cm) of 24g copper wire

5' (152.5 cm) of 28g copper wire

1 copper round, 2mm

1 crystal briolette, 11x10mm

1 crystal bicone, 6mm

3 crystal bicones, 4mm

35½" (90 cm) of copper 1.4mm cable chain

TOOLS

Ruler

Flush cutters or wire cutters

Round-nose pliers

Tile

Protective eyewear

Cross-locking tweezers

Butane micro torch

Quenching bowl

Pickling solution

Fine-point permanent marker

Steel ring-sizing mandrel

Flat-nose pliers

Chain-nose pliers

Painter's tape

Round #2 pencil or 7mm dowel

Chasing hammer

Steel bench block

Needle files

Beading awl

Liver of sulfur

#0000 extra-fine steel wool

Soft brass wire bristle brush or toothbrush

Polishing cloth (optional)

Tumbler (optional)

anila
LARIAT NECKLACE

Perfect your freeform shaping with this classical design with a wire-woven twist.

level ⇒ **INTERMEDIATE**

finished size ⇒ ⁹⁄₁₆" wide x 1⅝" high (14.2 mm x 4.1 cm)

length ⇒ 36½" (92.5 cm)

cutting and balling the wire

1 Cut 4" (10 cm) of 16g wire. Using round-nose pliers, make a loop on one end just big enough to easily slip the chain through.

2 Cut 4" (10 cm) of 18g wire. Place the tile on your work surface and put on the protective eyewear. Using cross-locking tweezers to hold the wire, use the micro torch to ball up one end. Quench. Cut 2" (5 cm) of 18g wire and ball up both ends; the finished length should be close to 1¾" (4.5 cm). Pickle the copper wire and mark the 1¾" (4.5 cm) length of wire ¾" (2 cm) in from one of the balled ends with the permanent marker.

weaving

3 Hold the 16g wire so the loop is facing away from you. Place the balled end of the 4" (10 cm) 18g wire to the right of the 16g wire.

4 Leaving a 4" (10 cm) tail, use the 28g wire to weave both wires using the modified soumak weave, weaving ¼–½" (6 mm–1.3 cm) from the loop. *note: We do this so we have wires to grip as we start out the weave. Once the weave is started, we will push the weave down.* Weave for three rows and stop. Flip the form over and coil around the 18g wire three times with the 4" (10 cm) tail. Use your fingers to pull the base wires down, moving the weave, until the weave reaches the loop and balled end. Trim the excess 28g wire from the 4" (10 cm) tail.

5 Flip the woven form so the loop is at the bottom with the 18g wire on the right. Add the second 18g wire to the left of the 16g wire with the ¾" (2 cm) mark at the top. Begin weaving all three wires together with the remaining 28g wire. Stop weaving at the ¾" (2 cm) mark, finishing the weave on a short row, around the 16g wire. *note: You should have a 1" (2.5 cm) woven piece.* Trim the 28g wire, leaving a 6" (15 cm) tail **(Fig. 1)**.

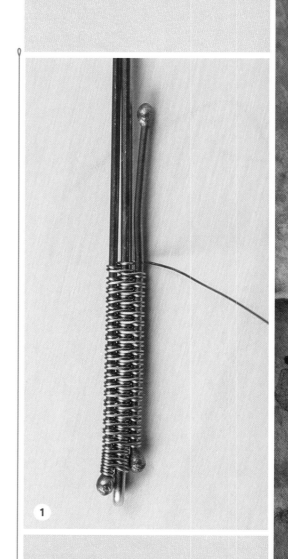

1

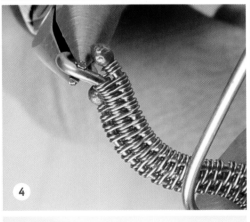

forming

6 Using your fingers, bend the woven form around the tip of the ring mandrel, starting with the looped end and creating a half circle. Using your thumb, curve the last bit of weave away from the ring mandrel as shown **(Fig. 2)**.

7 Using flat-nose pliers, chain-nose pliers, or your fingers, twist the end of the weave so the base wires face toward you **(Fig. 3)**. *tip: Be careful not to break or mar the weave with the pliers by squeezing the pliers too tightly. You may also want to cover the weave with painter's tape to help protect it from tool marks.* Using chain-nose pliers, bend the loop toward the shorter balled end wire on the left **(Fig. 4)**.

8 Flip the woven form so the unballed end of the longer 18g wire is on the left. The base wires will now be referred to by number: the 4" (10 cm) 18g wire is Wire 1, followed by Wires 2 and 3.

9 Separate the base wires so Wire 1 is to the left and Wires 2 and 3 are to the right. Place the 7mm dowel between Wires 1 and 2 and then bend Wire 2 around the dowel so it crosses over itself where the weave ends.

10 Using your fingers, curve Wire 2 in toward the weave **(Fig. 5)**. Using the back of the round-nose pliers, create a simple loop on the end of Wire 2 that faces toward the weave. Cut the loop in half at the top.

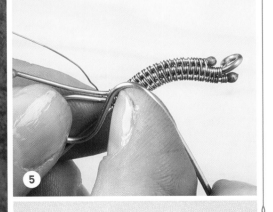

11 Push Wire 2 away from the weave. Using the chasing hammer and steel bench block, hammer a paddle on the end of the wire and then round the edges of the paddle with the file. Reposition the wire so it is back over the weave (**Fig. 6**).

12 Bend Wire 3 (now on the left) up toward the weave, making sure that Wire 1 (far right) is not under the loop of Wire 2. Flare out (see page 32) the bottom of the loop on Wire 2 with the hammer.

13 Position Wire 1 under Wire 2. Using the back of the round-nose pliers, form a loop on Wire 1 next to the loop on Wire 2 (**Fig. 7**). Using your fingers, bend Wire 1 so it follows the same curve as Wire 2. Organically loop Wire 1 to create a loop at the last curve on Wire 1. Trim the excess wire, leaving the loop open as shown (**Fig. 8**).

14 Using the tip of the round-nose pliers, create a small loop at the base of the weave with Wire 3 and curve the length of the wire across Wires 1 and 2 (**Fig. 9**). Use the round-nose pliers to curve the balled end inward, so it sits inside the loop of Wire 2 as shown.

To wear the necklace, position the woven form so Wire 1 is on the bottom; otherwise, it will flip. Slip the necklace on and pull the 4mm bicone end of chain around the back of your neck for a second time and through the largest loop. Pull the chain until the 6mm bicone passes through the loop. Adjust the length of the chain to achieve different looks.

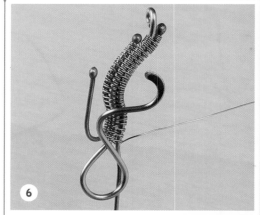

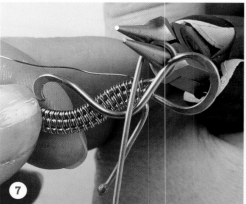

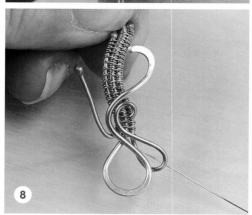

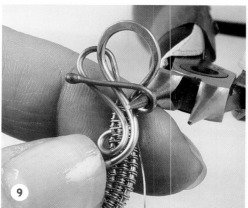

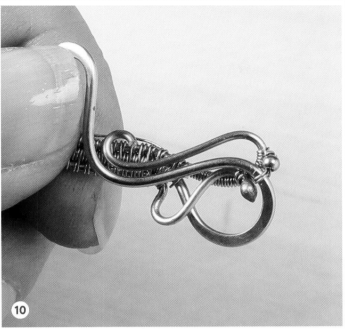

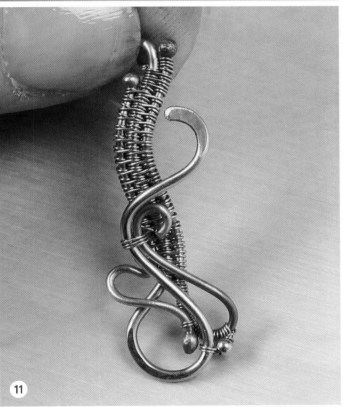

15 Flip the woven form so the back is facing up. Use the remaining 28g wire, not the tail, to coil Wire 1, starting at the weave; stop coiling when you reach the balled end of Wire 3.

16 Flip the woven form over so the front is facing up. Lash Wires 1 and 3 together twice. Continue to coil Wire 1 until there's enough space to add one copper round between Wires 1 and 2.

17 Thread one copper round onto the 28g wire and bring the wire over to Wire 2. Wrap twice around Wire 2 and then pass back through the bead. Wrap once around Wire 1 before securing the 28g wire around the wires passing through the round. Trim the 28g wire flush **(Fig. 10)**.

18 On the opposite end, use the beading awl to puncture the weave between Wires 2 (center) and 3 (left), inside the loop on Wire 1. Make the hole large enough to thread the 28g wire through three times, but be careful not to damage the weave when making the hole.

19 Thread the 28g wire tail from the back, through the hole, and to the front. Lash Wires 1 and 2 to the weave twice, ending on the back. Pass the 28g wire through the hole for the third time, to the front, so the 28g wire is behind Wires 1 and 2 and next to the lashings. Secure the 28g wire around the outside of the lashings; trim the excess wire **(Fig. 11)**.

final touches

20 Cut 32" (81.5 cm) from the chain. Using the 24g wire, begin making a wrapped loop on the briolette, attaching the loop to one end of the chain before completing the wrapped loop. Wrap the remaining 24g wire down around the tip of the briolette and back up around the loop. Thread the other end of the chain first through the largest loop on the pendant and then through the small loop on the other end **(Fig. 12)**.

21 To create a crystal bicone link, cut 3" (7.5 cm) of 22g wire and center the 6mm crystal bicone on the wire. Begin a wrapped loop on each end of the wire but don't wrap them closed. Attach the free end of the 32" (81.5 cm) chain to one loop; complete the wrap. Cut 2¼" (5.5 cm) from the remaining 3½" (9 cm) length of chain. Attach the second loop to one end of the 2¼" (5.5 cm) chain; complete the wrap. *tip: This 6mm crystal bicone will help act as a stopper for the necklace, so it needs to be big enough to just barely slip through the largest loop in the woven form.*

22 Cut the 2¼" (5.5 cm) chain 1" (2.5 cm) from the bottom link. Cut 2" (5 cm) of 22g wire and center a 4mm crystal bicone on the wire. Begin a wrapped loop on each end. Attach one loop to the free end of the 2¼" (5.5 cm) chain and attach the second loop to one end of the 1" (2.5 cm) chain; complete the wraps.

23 Cut 2" (5 cm) of 22g wire and begin a second 4mm crystal bicone link. Attach one loop to one end of the remaining ¾" (2 cm) length of chain and attach the second loop to the free end of the 1" (2.5 cm) chain; complete the wraps. Cut 2" (5 cm) of 22g wire and ball one end, creating a head pin. Thread the remaining 4mm crystal bicone onto the head pin and begin a wrapped loop. Attach the loop to the free end of the ¾" (2 cm) chain; complete the wrap.

24 Oxidize the necklace with liver of sulfur. Polish with the steel wool and brass brush. Use a polishing cloth or a tumbler to clean and brighten the jewelry.

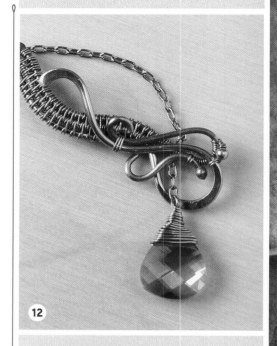

12

variation

This necklace is beautiful in silver with purple pearls. When making your own variation, remember that both ends of the chain need the proper weight. On one end, use an 11mm or larger briolette with enough weight on its own. On the other end, use smaller beads that can slip through the loop. You will need to add several links onto the end of the chain to create enough of a counterweight to keep the chain from moving when the necklace is worn.

TECHNIQUES

Modified Soumak Weave (page 24)

Loops (page 27)

Forming (page 21)

Hammering (page 32)

Lashing (page 18)

Embellishing (page 35)

Filing (page 33)

MATERIALS

4" (10 cm) of 16g copper wire

13" (33 cm) of 18g copper wire

12" (30.5 cm) of 22g copper wire

10' (3 m) of 28g copper wire

3" (7.5 cm) of 28g copper wire (scrap wire)

6" (15 cm) of 30g copper wire

1 vitrail medium crystal teardrop pendant, 24mm

1 copper round, 2mm

2 pink crystal bicones, 4mm

2 copper rounds, 3mm

14½" (37 cm) of copper 1x2mm flat oval chain

Simple S-clasp (see page 43 for materials and instructions)

TOOLS

Ruler

Flush cutters or wire cutters

Fine-point permanent marker

Stainless steel ring-sizing mandrel

Round-nose pliers

Chasing hammer

Steel bench block

Needle file

Painter's tape

Chain-nose pliers

Liver of sulfur

#0000 extra-fine steel wool

Brass wire bristle brush or toothbrush

Polishing cloth (optional)

Tumbler (optional)

raindrop
PENDANT

Make a fitted frame for a teardrop crystal with cascading swirls down the side.

level ⇒ **INTERMEDIATE**

finished size ⇒ ¾" wide x 1⅞" high (2 x 4.7 cm)

length ⇒ 16¾" (42.5 cm)

cutting and forming the wire

1 Cut 4" (10 cm) of 16g wire. Mark the center of the wire with the permanent marker. Center the mark at size 1 on the ring mandrel and form the wire around the mandrel to form a "U" shape. Make sure the two "arms" of the wire are equal in length.

2 Place the teardrop crystal inside the U-shaped wire and form the wire around the crystal to create a fitted frame. At the tip of the crystal, bend the wire arms straight up and parallel to each other **(Fig. 1)**.

3 Trim the right arm ¼" (6 mm) from the end of the wire and the other arm ⅜" (1 cm) from the end of the wire. Using round-nose pliers, bend the end of each wire so it curves outward. Use the chasing hammer and steel bench block to flare out the curved bottom and create a paddle on each of the wire ends. Round the paddles with the file **(Fig. 2)**.

4 Cut 8" (20.5 cm) of 18g wire. Mark the center of the wire and center that mark at size 4 on the ring mandrel. Create a U-shaped wire as in Step 1. Cut 5" (12.5 cm) of 18g wire and using round-nose pliers, make an open loop with a loose spiral on one end of the wire.

weaving

5 Place the 16g wire "U" shape inside the 18g wire "U" shape, with the center marks lined up and the longer 16g wire paddle on the right. Tape the left half of the frame together. Starting in the middle of the 28g wire, begin weaving the two wires together at the center marks using the modified soumak weave. Using your fingers, shape the right arm of the 18g wire so it follows the curves of the 16g wire as you weave. Continue to weave up the right side, stopping the weave at the top of the "U," where the left and right arms would touch if pinched together **(Fig. 3)**.

6 Remove the tape. Shape the arm of the 18g wire on the left so it curves around the 16g wire and then weave the left side of the frame. *tip: Remember that you can flip the frame to keep the weaving motion fluid and natural.* Stop the weave when it's even with the weave on the right side.

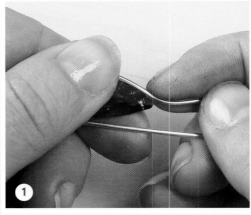

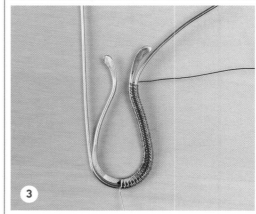

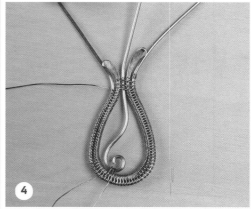

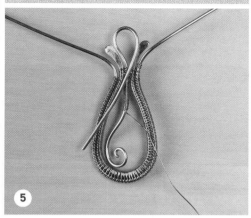

5

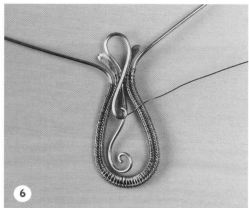

6

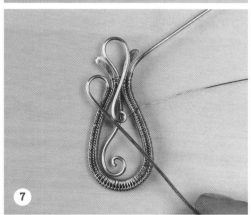

7

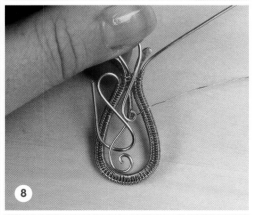

8

7 Take the 5" (12.5 cm) 18g wire from Step 4 and place the loop on the bottom left inside the woven frame as shown. Use a scrap piece of 28g wire to temporarily secure it to the base. *note: Painter's tape would not secure the 18g wire enough for us to further shape the wire. It would also get in the way of the shaping that we will be doing.* Using your fingers, bend and curve the straight part of the 18g wire so it sits between the two woven arms, with a gentle wave shaped into the 18g wire. The five base wires will now be referenced beginning with the 18g wire on the far left as Wire 1, followed by Wires 2, 3, 4, and 5. Wire 2 has the shorter 16g paddle.

8 Take the right 28g wire and weave Wires 2, 3, 4, and 5 together for three rows, stopping the weave on Wire 5. Coil the 28g wire around Wire 5 three times and trim **(Fig. 4)**. Bend Wire 3 slightly to the left so it follows the curve of the paddle on Wire 2.

forming

9 Remove the scrap wire holding the 18g loop to the frame. Use the bottom left 28g wire to coil down Wire 3 for ⅜" (1 cm). Using the back of the round-nose pliers, form a loop at the top of Wire 3 and then bring the wire around so it crosses over the front of the weave as shown **(Fig. 5)**. *tip: The loop should be higher than Wire 4.* Organically loop the wire, with the loop forming just below the coils. Trim the excess wire **(Fig. 6)**.

10 Using your fingers, bend Wire 1 outward and down into a loop, bringing the end of the wire across the frame as shown **(Fig. 7)**. Shape Wire 1 into a loose loop around Wire 3 by bringing the end of Wire 1 around and behind the bottom of Wire 3 **(Fig. 8)**.

Continue to loosely wrap around Wire 3 to form a large loop **(Fig. 9)**. Trim the end of Wire 1 just as it begins to curve on the left inside of the woven frame **(Fig. 10)**.

11 Using your fingers, push Wire 5 behind Wire 4 so it sits between Wires 3 and 4. Use the chain-nose pliers to bend Wire 5 over to the front of the frame, with the bend just above the paddled end of Wire 4 and with the bend even with the top of the loop in Wire 3 **(Fig. 11)**. With your fingers, curve Wire 5 in a gentle arc across the top loop on Wire 1, and then curve it back just below the top open loop on Wire 3 and over to the right side of the woven frame.

12 Using round-nose pliers, create a slight downward curve on Wire 5 below the open loop on Wire 3 as shown. Trim to the desired length **(Fig. 12)**. Push Wire 5 to the right and away from the woven frame. Use the chasing hammer and steel bench block to create a paddle on the end of the wire. Round the paddle with the file.

To adjust this pendant to fit different sizes of teardrop beads, use the ring mandrel to make the perfect fit with the 16g wire. Drop three ring sizes down on the mandrel to shape the outer 18g wire.

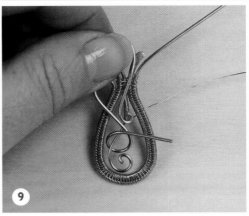

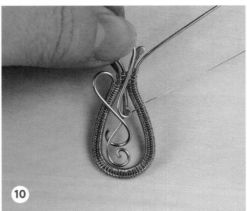

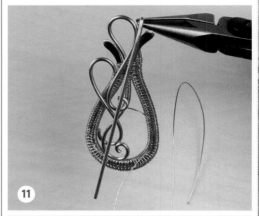

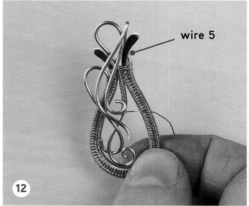

wire 5

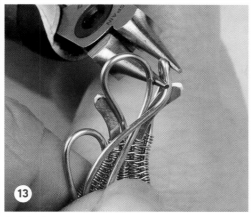

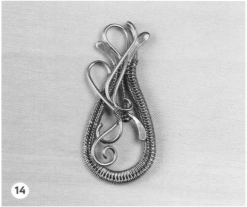

back view

13 Reposition Wire 5 back over the woven form. Using round-nose pliers, grasp the bend on Wire 5 and curve it toward the top loop on Wire 3 **(Fig. 13)**.

14 Bring the 28g wire coiled around Wire 3 in Step 9 over Wire 5 and over the open loop on Wire 3. Lash Wires 3 and 1 together three times. Continue coiling down just Wire 1 five times.

embellishing

15 String one 2mm round onto the end of the coiled 28g wire from Step 14. Bring the 28g wire over to the paddled end of Wire 5 and wrap twice around Wire 5. Thread the 28g wire back through the round and wrap once around Wire 1. Secure the 28g wire twice around the wires passing through the round (shown on the left side of the round). Trim the 28g wire flush in the back **(Fig. 14)**.

16 Thread the crystal teardrop onto the 30g wire and center it. Place the teardrop inside the woven frame. Bring each 30g around the outside of the frame and then pass back through the teardrop. Repeat, but this time, wrap the 30g wire around the other arm before threading through the teardrop. Do this two more times so that each arm woven has the 30g wire wrapped around it twice. Secure the 30g wire in the back of the pendant by wrapping each 30g tail twice around the wires passing through the teardrop. Trim the excess 30g wire **(Fig. 15)**.

17 Cut the 22g into four 3" (7.5 cm) pieces. Begin a wrapped loop on one end of each wire but do not wrap the loop. Cut the chain in half. Thread the partially wrapped loops onto the four ends of the two chains. Complete the wrapped loops. String one 4mm crystal onto two of the looped wires and one 3mm copper round onto the last two wires. Begin a second wrapped loop on the other end of the wires, except make one of the copper round loops large enough for the end of the clasp to fit through. Complete the wrap on the larger loop only. Attach the crystal loops to the top loop on the pendant and complete the wraps. Attach the loop on the last copper round to the loop on the clasp; complete the wrap.

18 Oxidize the finished necklace with liver of sulfur. Polish with the steel wool and brass wire bristle brush. Use a polishing cloth or a tumbler to clean and brighten the jewelry.

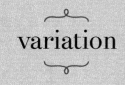

variation

Use a blue 12mm coin pearl with silver wire to create this variation (right). Tip: If you don't want to risk damaging the pearl in the liver of sulfur, you can use pre-oxidized wire to attach the pearl after the necklace has been oxidized. Use a bright blue crystal teardrop to create this variation (left).

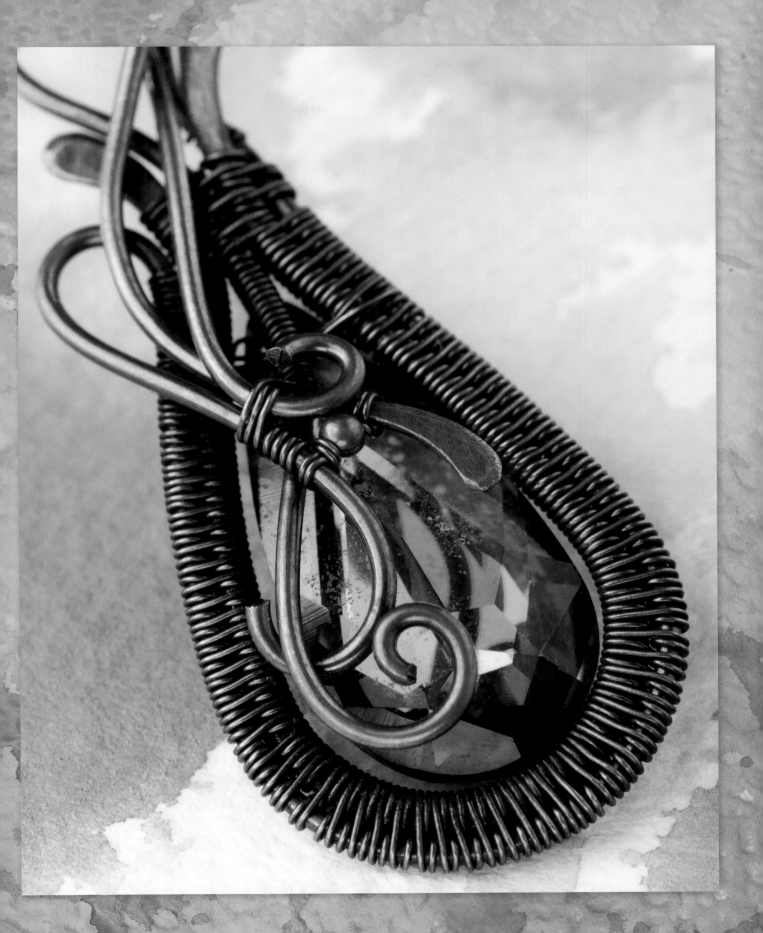

MATERIALS

65" (165 cm) of 16g copper wire

20' (6.1 m) of 28g copper wire

20' (6.1 m) of 30g fine silver wire

TOOLS

Flush cutters or wire cutters

Fine-point permanent marker

Ruler

4 bobbins

Painter's tape

Needle files

Round-nose pliers

Round #2 pencil or 7mm dowel

Chain-nose pliers

Beading awl

Bracelet mandrel

Rawhide mallet

Flat-nose pliers

Chasing hammer

Steel bench block

Live of sulfur

#0000 extra-fine steel wool

Soft brass wire bristle brush or toothbrush

Polishing cloth (optional)

Tumbler (optional)

all checkered out
BRACELET

Each weave has its own texture; by combining them we can get interesting patterns. You can make this pattern bold by mixing metals or give it a subtle touch by using the same metal.

level ⇒ **INTERMEDIATE**

length ⇒ 7¼" (18.5 cm)

cutting and marking the wire

1 Cut six 10" (25.5 cm) pieces of 16g wire. Mark the center of each wire with the permanent marker. Cut 5" (12.5 cm) of 16g wire and mark the center; fold it in half at the mark.

2 Coil the full length of 28g wire onto two bobbins (10' [3 m] onto each bobbin), starting at the ends and meeting in the middle. Repeat with the 30g wire.

weaving

3 Tape the six 10" (25.5 cm) pieces together at the center mark, leaving enough room between the base wires to slip the 28g wire through. The base wires will now be referenced by number: the far left wire is Wire 1 followed by Wires 2, 3, 4, 5, and 6.

4 Starting in the middle of the 28g wire, weave all six wires together using the modified soumak weave. Weave one row of short wraps. Continue weaving Wires 4, 5, and 6 together for five rows. *tip: I like to count my long wraps to help keep track of how many rows I have.* Stop the weave after making a long wrap around Wire 4, ending with the wire on the front, between Wires 4 and 5.

5 Thread the middle of the 30g wire between Wires 3 and 4 (**Fig. 1**). *note: Because the 28g wire has already secured the base wires together, you will not need a starter row with the 30g wire.* Begin weaving Wires 3, 2, and 1 together with the 30g wire using the basic figure-eight weave. Weave these three wires together until you are even with the modified soumak weave. Stop the weave between Wires 2 and 3 with the 30g wire in the back. *note: For this design, it's important that the 30g wire always ends in the back.*

6 Using the 28g wire, continue the modified soumak weave by bringing the wire across to Wire 3. Weave Wires 1, 2, and 3 together for five rows. Stop the weave between Wires 2 and 3 as shown, with the 28g wire in the back (**Fig. 2**).

7 Bring the 30g wire from the back and thread it between Wires 3 and 4. Weave Wires 4, 5, and 6 with the 30g wire using the basic figure-eight weave. Stop the weave when you are even with the modified soumak weave. The 30g wire should be between Wires 4 and 5, and in the back.

8 Use the 28g wire to continue the modified soumak weave, bringing the wire across to Wire 4 and weaving Wires 4, 5, and 6 together for five rows. Stop the weave between Wires 4 and 5, with the 28g wire in the front.

9 Bring the 30g wire from the back and thread it between Wires 3 and 4. Weave Wires 1, 2, and 3 with the basic figure-eight weave. Continue this pattern of alternating between the two weaves for a total of eleven rows of checkered modified soumak weave squares.

10 After you have completed the eleventh row of squares, finish the weave on this end with three rows of modified soumak weave using the 28g wire and weaving all six wires together.

11 Remove the tape and repeat the pattern, weaving eleven more rows of checkered squares to complete the weave. Trim the 30g wire flush to the weave.

shaping the base wires

12 Trim Wire 1 to ½" (1.3 cm) and file flat. Using round-nose pliers, create a simple loop on Wire 1, with the loop facing outward.

13 Bend Wire 2 around the curve of the loop on Wire 1, and parallel to the weave. Bend Wire 3 to the left and mark the wire ¾" (2 cm) above the weave. Using the #2 pencil (or 7mm dowel) as a mandrel, bend Wire 3 around the pencil (centering the ¾" [2 cm] mark at the top of the loop), and continue around until Wire 3 crosses in front of the loop on Wire 1. Open the loop on Wire 1 and bend the arm of Wire 3 around the inside the loop and to the back (**Fig. 3**). Reposition the loop on Wire 1. Trim Wire 3

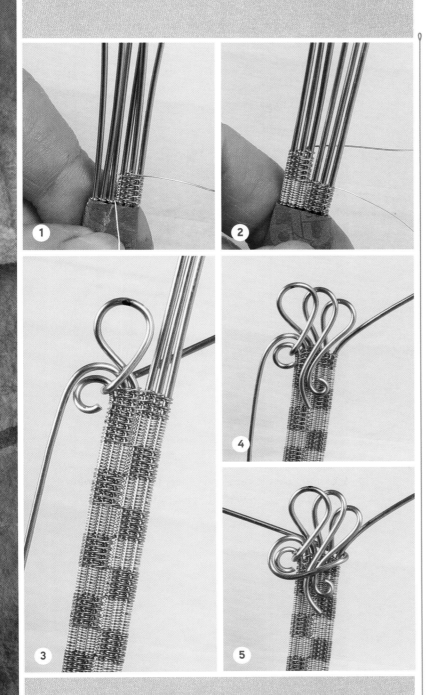

on the back, between Wires 1 and 2. Using chain-nose pliers, tuck the end of Wire 3 between Wires 1 and 2. Compress Wire 3 around Wire 1.

14 Bend Wire 4 to the left (just behind Wire 3) and organically shape a large loop that is a little smaller than the preceding loop in Wire 3. *tip: Because Wire 4 sits behind the loop of Wire 3, it would be awkward to use round-nose pliers or a dowel in place of your fingers.* Cross the arm of Wire 4 over the weave and below the loop on Wire 1.

15 Create a loop on Wire 5 as you did with Wire 4, making sure the new loop is smaller than the previous loop. The new loop should sit behind and below Wire 4. Cross the arm of Wire 5 in front of the weave. Organically loop the wire, making a simple loop facing outward. *tip: The bottom of the loop should line up with the bottom of the first checkered square.* Trim the excess wire so the loop is open.

16 Bend the arm of Wire 4 so it follows the curve of Wire 5. Trim Wire 4 below the loop on Wire 5 **(Fig. 4)**.

17 Bend Wire 2 so it curves around the loop on Wire 1, across the weave, and over Wires 4 and 5. Bend Wire 2 up behind Wire 6 to the back of the bracelet **(Fig. 5)**. Trim Wire 2 on the back between Wires 5 and 6. Using chain-nose pliers, compress Wire 2 around Wire 6.

18 Create a loop on Wire 6 that is smaller than the previous loop and sits in back of Wire 5, below it. Bring the arm of Wire 6 across the front of Wires 4 and 5 and below the arm of Wire 2. Organically loop the wire, making a simple loop on Wire 6, with the bottom of the loop lining up with the bottom of the second checkered square on the left side of the bracelet. Trim the excess wire so the loop is open as shown **(Fig. 6)**.

19 Use the beading awl to puncture the weave between Wires 3 and 4 where Wires 2 and 6 touch; the hole needs to be large enough to pass through twice. Cut the 28g wire, leaving a 6" (15 cm) tail. Thread the 28g wire from the back through the hole. Lash Wires 2 and 6 together three times. Thread the 28g wire through the hole to the back.

20 Puncture the weave between Wires 1 and 2, passing the beading awl through the end loop on Wire 6. *note: This hole needs to be large enough to thread the 28g wire through three times.* Thread the 28g wire from the back through the hole and lash the loop on Wire 6 to the side of the weave twice. Secure the 28g wire on the side of the bracelet, wrapping it twice through the lashing just made. If needed, enlarge the opening slightly with the beading awl. *tip: You will be wrapping perpendicular to the lashings.* Trim the excess wire **(Fig. 7)**.

21 Repeat Steps 12–20 to shape the base wires on the other end of the bracelet.

22 Place the weave over the bracelet mandrel and use the rawhide mallet to shape it around the mandrel. Adjust the bracelet if needed so it fits comfortably around your wrist.

Make sure the base wires are straight and close together. Remember that a complete row with the modified soumak weave consists of a row of short wraps and a row of long wraps.

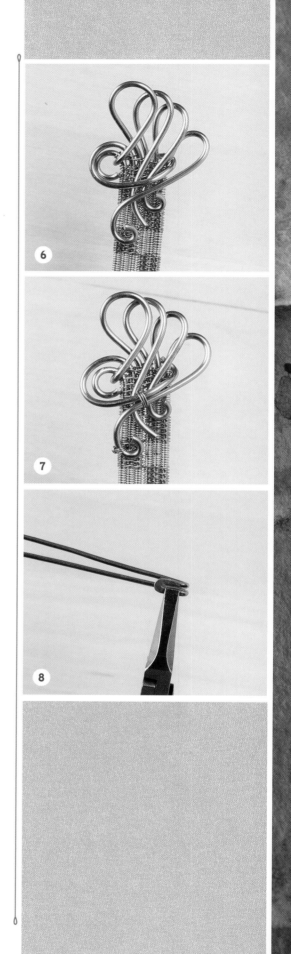

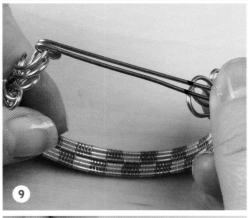

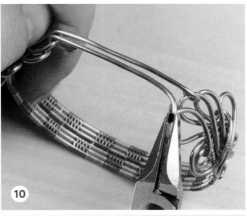

finishing touches

23 Mark the folded wire from Step 1 at ¼" (6 mm) from the fold with the permanent marker. Using the chasing hammer and steel bench block, hammer the tip of the fold, making sure not hammer beyond the ¼" (6 mm) mark.

24 Using flat-nose pliers, grasp one arm of the wire at the ¼" (6 mm) mark and bend the wire over the top jaw of the pliers, creating one side of the hook. Repeat on the other arm of the wire, making sure both arms line up next to each other **(Fig. 8)**.

25 Test-fit the hook to make sure it can slip onto the largest loop on the end of the bracelet. With the hook inside the loop, position the end of the arms over the largest loop at the other end of the bracelet. Mark the arms where they cross the loop as shown **(Fig. 9)**.

26 Measure another ¼" (6 mm) from the mark and trim the wire ends. Using the round-nose pliers, create a simple loop on the end of the wires, with the loops facing inward, toward the hook. *tip: The simple loops need to be large to rotate freely around the loop on the bracelet.*

27 Open the simple loops and slip them onto the large loops on Wires 3 and 4. Close the simple loops. Using flat-nose pliers, bend the simple loop attached to Wire 3 outward as shown **(Fig. 10)**. *note: This will straighten the arm so it lines up properly on the other side.*

28 Oxidize the bracelet with liver of sulfur and polish with the steel wool and the brass brush. Use a polishing cloth or a tumbler to clean and give a brighter finish to the jewelry.

TECHNIQUES

Modified Soumak Weave (page 24)

Forming (page 21)

Hammering (page 32)

Filing (page 33)

MATERIALS

3" (7.5 cm) of 14g fine silver wire

4" (10 cm) of 16g fine silver wire

18" (45.5 cm) of 18g fine silver wire

8" (20.5 cm) of 20g dead-soft sterling silver wire

20' (6.1 m) of 30g fine silver wire

TOOLS

Ruler

Flush cutters or wire cutters

Needle file

Fine-point permanent marker

Stainless steel-ring sizing mandrel

Rawhide mallet

Steel bench block

Chasing hammer

Flat-nose pliers

Round-nose pliers

Painter's tape

Liver of sulfur

#0000 extra-fine steel wool

Brass wire bristle brush or toothbrush

Polishing cloth (optional)

Tumbler (optional)

scorpio
EARRINGS

Originally designed to be flat hoops, these earrings have a three-dimensional curve, thanks to a ring mandrel. This simple step transformed the design from ordinary to extraordinary.

level ⇒ **INTERMEDIATE**

finished size ⇒ ⅞" wide x 2½" high (2.2 x 6.5 cm)

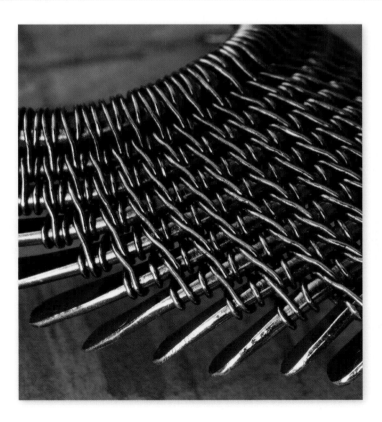

cutting and forming the wire

1 Cut two 1½" (3.8 cm) pieces of 14g wire and file the ends flat. Mark the center of each wire with the permanent marker. Center one wire at the size 4 mark on the ring mandrel. Use the rawhide mallet to form the wire around the mandrel. Repeat with the second wire. Place each wire on the steel bench block and use the chasing hammer to create a paddle on the wire ends, making sure not to distort the curved shape **(Fig. 1)**. Smooth and round all the paddled ends with the file.

2 Cut two 2" (5 cm) pieces of 16g wire and file one end flat. Mark each wire at ¾" (2 cm) and 1" (2.5 cm) from the filed end. Using flat-nose pliers, grasp one wire at the ¾" (2 cm) mark, with the ¾" (2 cm) length sticking out on the left side of the pliers. Use your thumb to bend the left side of the wire up against the jaw of the pliers, creating a 90° angle. Grasp the wire at the 1" (2.5 cm) mark, with the 1" (2.5 cm) length sticking out the right side of the pliers, and bend the wire up to create another 90° angle. Repeat with the second wire **(Fig. 2)**.

3 Trim the ends of the longer arms to ⅞" (2.2 cm) and loop the end outward. With your round-nose pliers, gently arc the tip of the other arm outward to make a tail. Check to make sure your two 16g wires are shaped the same.

4 Use the chasing hammer and steel bench block to flare the outside of the loops, create a paddle on the tails, and flatten the 90° angles at the top of each wire. Use the file to smooth and round the tails **(Fig. 3)**.

> It is critical that you are precise in cutting your wire. Being a ¹⁄₁₆" (2 mm) off makes a big difference in how the paddles line up on the sides. They should make a gradual descent from top to bottom, especially in the front, where they're most noticeable.

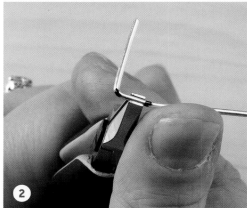

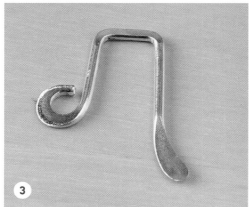

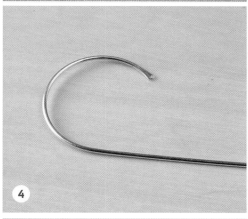

4

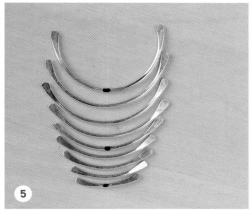

5

5 Cut two 4" (10 cm) pieces of 20g wire. File one end flat on each wire. Starting at the flat end, form one wire around the ring mandrel at the size 7 mark, creating a "C" shape. Use the rawhide mallet to ensure the wire is well formed around the mandrel. Repeat for the second wire. Use the chasing hammer and steel bench block to create a paddle on the filed end of each wire **(Fig. 4)**.

6 Cut the following lengths of 18g wire: two 1½" (3.8 cm) pieces, two 1⅜" (3.5 cm) pieces, two 1¼" (3.2 cm) pieces, two 1⅛" (2.9 cm) pieces, two 1" (2.5 cm) pieces, two ⅞" (2.2 cm) pieces, two ¾" (2 cm) pieces, two ⅝" (1.5 cm) pieces, and two ½" (1.3 cm) pieces. Mark the centers of wires lengths 1½" (3.8 cm), 1" (2.5 cm), and ½" (1.3 cm). Line the wires up in descending order, longest to shortest. Keep the individual lengths separated; it will be harder to see which wires are longer when we curve them.

7 Use the rawhide hammer to shape the 1½" (3.8 cm) lengths around the ring mandrel at the size 10 mark. Repeat with the 1⅜" (3.5 cm) lengths at the size 13 mark. Repeat with the remaining lengths of 18g wire at the size 16 mark.

8 Use the chasing hammer and steel bench block to create a paddle on the tips of all the lengths of 18g wire, about ⅛" (3 mm) in. *note: For your first pair, I suggest that you lightly paddle the ends, as this will make it easier to weave around. The wider the paddle, the more difficult it becomes to weave around because the paddles will begin to overlap each other* **(Fig. 5)**.

In this design, the finer texture of the 30g wire looks better than 28g wire, but if you find it challenging to use, switch to the thicker wire.

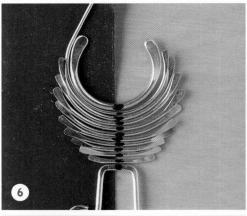

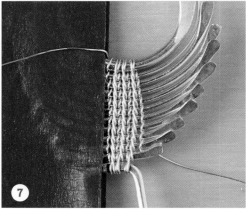

Weaving with twelve base wires will cause the weave to zigzag. Stop every row and compress the wires to keep the weave straight.

assembling the wires

9 Separate all the wire pieces into two equal sets with the 18g wires organized in descending size and kept flat on your work surface. *note: You will only be using one set for the rest of the instructions, completing one earring.*

10 Tear off 2" (5 cm) of painter's tape and lay it flat on your work surface with the sticky side facing up. *tip: Fold the ends over to the back, nonsticky side, to create a sticky surface that will stick to your work surface. This will keep the tape flat and in place as you lay down and position the twelve wires.* Place one 14g wire on the tape with the center mark on the wire lined up with the edge of the tape and with the paddled ends facing up.

11 Place one 20g wire below the 14g wire with the paddled end of the 20g wire just below the right paddled end of the 14g wire.

12 Add the 18g wires, starting with the longest and descending to the shortest, making sure each wire is centered with the 14g wire and all the paddles are facing up. Use the center marks on three of the 18g wires to help you line up the remaining 18g wires. *note: After the fourth wire, widen the arc in the curve by hand, by pulling the paddled ends apart. This reshapes the curve so you can properly nestle the wires one below the other as you center each wire with the previous one. Remember, we want the width of one 30g wire between each wire. The last ½" (1.3 cm) wire when reshaped will become a straight line with paddles curving up.*

13 Center the 16g wire below the smallest 18g wire. Using the permanent marker, draw a line down the center of the earring so all wires have a center mark **(Fig. 6)**.

14 Place another 2" (5 cm) piece of painter's tape on top of the wires, making sure the center line is still visible. Press the tape down to secure the wires between the both pieces of tape. The impression of the wires within will be visible.

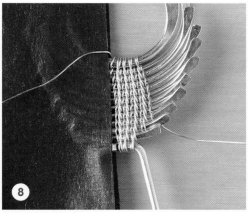

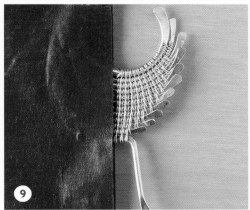

weaving

15 Cut 10' (3 m) of 30g wire; starting 5' (1.5 m) in, slip the 30g wire between the 14g wire and the 20g wire. You should have a 5' (1.5 m) working wire and a 5' (1.5 m) tail. *note: The wires will now be referenced by number, starting with the 14g wire as Wire 1 and ending with the 16g wire as Wire 12.*

16 Using the modified soumak weave, begin weaving all twelve wires together down the center of the earring. Stop frequently to compact the weave. *note: Chances are that there will be a gap a little larger than a 30g wire between the base wires. If so, nudge the wires with your fingernail to bring them closer together as you weave.* Continue weaving until you reach the bend in Wire 12. Stop the weave and check that all the wires are lined up down the center. If not, remove the tape and adjust the wires **(Fig. 7)**. *note: The base wires can easily shift as you weave. Keep the center marks lined up and make sure the paddles are lined up properly in descending order.*

17 As you weave, the paddles will begin to overlap. It is easier to position the paddles so each paddle is slightly on top of the wire above it. (This will be the back of the earring.) Use your fingernails to lift a paddle to slip the 30g wire through if it becomes stuck. Do not force it around the paddles because this can cause it to break. Continue the weave, but this time, decrease the weave by omitting the two bottom base wires, Wires 11 and 12. Weave Wires 1–10 together for one row **(Fig. 8)**.

18 At the next row, decrease again and weave only Wires 1–9. Continue to decrease every row until you reach Wire 3.

19 Weave Wires 1, 2, and 3 together for two rows before decreasing to Wire 2.

20 Weave Wires 1 and 2 together for five rows. Secure the 30g wire by wrapping it around Wire 2 four times. Trim the excess **(Fig. 9)**.

21 Remove the tape and flip the weave over. With the remaining 5' (1.5 m) of 30g wire, finish weaving the other side in the same manner. Wire 12 should have a total of five or six woven rows. Set aside.

22 Begin working on the second earring. Use the first earring as a reference to make sure that Wire 2, Wire 12, and the overlapping paddles of the second earring are a mirror image of the first.

shaping the ear wire

23 On both earrings, hand-shape the 20g wire to form a wide arc over the earring. Trim the excess below Wire 4. File smooth **(Fig. 10)**.

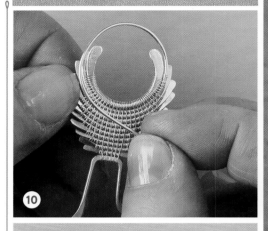

24 With the flat-nose pliers, bend the tip out. Hammer the tip and the arc.

25 Before molding the woven form, make sure the paddles overlap correctly. The paddles should be tucked behind the wire above it. (This is the front.) **(Fig. 11)**

three-dimensional forming

26 Center the woven form over the ring mandrel at the 10 mark, with the 16g wire pointing toward the tip of the ring mandrel.

27 With your fingers, press the woven form against the ring mandrel, giving it an arched shape.

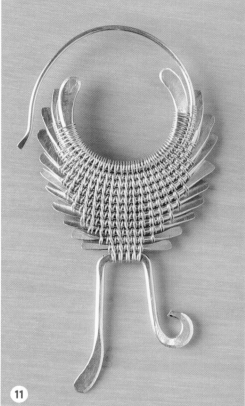

28 With the rawhide mallet, gently hammer the paddled ends around the ring mandrel, being careful around the weave **(Fig. 12)**. *note: If you hammer too hard, you risk breaking the 30g wire. tip: This is a good time to use painter's tape to cover the earrings before hammering around the ring mandrel.*

You can use 22g sterling silver for the ear wires instead of 20g if you prefer or switch out the wire for half-hard wire. If you choose to use half-hard wire instead of dead-soft wire, remember that it has more spring to it and will need to be shaped around the size 5 mark of the mandrel instead of size 7.

29 The forming has rotated the paddles. If you like, use the flat-nose pliers to spread the paddles apart or leave them as they are **(Fig. 13)**.

finishing the earrings

30 Use flat-nose pliers to gently grip the tail of the 16g wire at the bend. With your thumb anchoring and pushing from the other side, bring the two wire arms together, creating a triangle with the loop overlapping the tail **(Fig. 14)**.

31 Slightly straighten the curve in the ear wire created when you molded the woven form over the ring mandrel so the earring can be slipped onto the ear.

32 Oxidize the earrings in liver of sulfur and polish using the steel wool and brass bristle brush. Use a polishing cloth or a tumbler to clean and brighten the jewelry.

Tumble the earrings by themselves. The bottom of the earrings are delicate, and you may break the weave holding the 16g wire if the loop hooks onto another piece of jewelry in the tumbler.

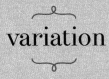

variation

Mix up the design elements. Instead of paddling the ends of the wire, create balled ends with a torch for a different look. See Balled Ends (page 33) for instructions on how to use a butane micro torch to create balled ends of wire.

TECHNIQUES

Basic Figure-Eight Weave (page 22)

Modified Soumak Weave (page 24)

Adding Base Wires (page 23)

Decreasing the Weave (page 24)

Puncturing the Weave (page 18)

Hammering (page 32)

Forming (page 21)

Lashing (page 18)

Coiling (page 35)

Loops (page 27)

MATERIALS

2¼" (5.5 cm) of 14g fine silver wire

8" (20.5 cm) of 18g fine silver wire

30" (76 cm) of 20g fine silver wire

8" (20.5 cm) of 22g fine silver wire

30' (9.1 m) of 30g fine silver wire on a spool or bobbin

2 lavender pearls, 6mm, with holes large enough to slip onto the 22g wire

French ear wires (see instructions and materials on page 41)

TOOLS

Ruler

Flush cutters or wire cutters

Needle files

Chasing hammer

Steel bench block

Fine-point permanent marker

Metal hole punch, 1.8mm

Flat-nose pliers

Ring mandrel

Beading awl

Round-nose pliers

Liver of sulfur

#0000 extra-fine steel wool

Soft brass wire bristle brush or toothbrush

Soft polishing cloth (optional)

Tumbler (optional)

feather
EARRINGS

These earrings are a wonderful example of the movement that can be captured when using the basic figure-eight weave. This look wouldn't be possible if we had used the modified soumak weave as the base weave instead of using it to secure the "V" wires.

level ⇒ **INTERMEDIATE**

finished size ⇒ 1⅛" wide x 3¼" high (2.8 x 8.5 cm)

cutting and forming the wire

1 Cut two 1⅛" (2.8 cm) pieces of 14g wire. File both ends flat. Using the chasing hammer and steel bench block, create a paddle on one end of each wire (see page 32). Hold the paddle end perpendicular to the bench block and create a paddle on the other end. Both paddles need to be between 3.5 and 4 mm wide. Mark the center of each paddle with the permanent marker. Use the 1.8mm hole punch to punch a hole through the center of the marks on the paddles. Use the file to remove any burrs from the punched holes and to round the edges of the paddle.

2 Cut two 4" (10 cm) pieces of 18g wire and mark the centers. Using flat-nose pliers, bend each wire at the mark to form a "V" shape with a 60° angle. Form each V-shaped wire around the tip of the ring mandrel as shown **(Fig. 1)**. Then curve the "arms" of the wires up so they are parallel. You should now have two leaf-shaped wires.

3 Cut ten 3" (7.5 cm) pieces of 20g wire. File the ends flat and mark the center of each wire. Using the chasing hammer, create paddles on all the ends. Using flat-nose pliers, bend each wire at the mark to create a "V" shape with about a 25° angle, making sure the paddles are facing each other and not facing you.

4 Cut two 4" (10 cm) pieces of 22g wire. Mark the wires 1⅛" (2.8 cm) from one end with the permanent marker. Using flat-nose pliers, bend each wire in half at the mark.

weaving

5 Take one 14g wire from Step 1 and mark ¼" (6 mm) from the tip of the paddle. Place one 20g V-shaped wire from Step 3 in back of the 14g wire as shown. The two arms of the "V" should be touching the mark on the 14g wire.

6 Leaving a 4" (10 cm) tail, use the 30g wire (from the spool or bobbin) to weave the three base wires together with the basic figure-eight weave.

7 Continue weaving, allowing space to form between the base wires as you weave. When you have created enough space between the base wires to add a new 20g V-shaped wire from Step 3, stop weaving, ending the weave on the left side as shown **(Fig. 2)**. *tip: I usually have enough room after about ⅛" (3 mm) of weave.*

adding base wires

8 Inspect the back of your work and make sure the "V" is not covering the hole of the 14g wire.

9 Place the new 20g V-shaped wire behind the 14g wire, so it nestles on either side of the 14g wire. To secure the new 20g wire to the 14g wire, bring the 30g wire across the back of Wire 1, the wire to the far left. Using the modified soumak weave, weave the new "V" wire to Wire 2, the 14g wire, before switching back to the basic figure-eight weave **(Fig. 3)**. *note: You will do this every time you add a new "V" wire as shown.* Continue weaving using the basic figure-eight weave.

10 The right arm of the new 20g V-shaped wire just added will be sticking out away from the other base wires. Gently push it into place so it lines up with the rest of the base wires. There are now five base wires (two 20g V-shaped wires and one 14g). *note: This will shift the numbering of the base wires. Every time we add an new "V" wire the base numbers will change to reflect this with Wire 1 always starting on the left followed by Wire 2.* If you have a noticeable gap between the weave where the new wire was added, this means that you added the wire too soon. There wasn't enough room between the base wires to add the new wire and fit the 30g wire. Back out of the weave, remove the "V" wire, and weave a few more rows before adding the "V" wire again. The gap can also mean that you are not compressing the weave after you have added the new wire.

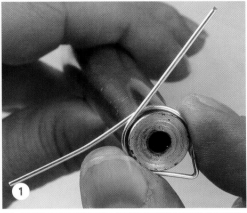

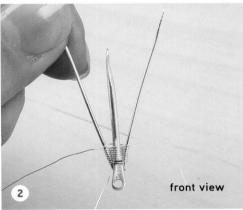

front view

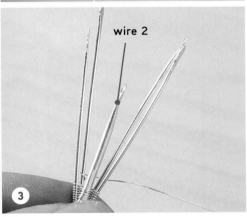

wire 2

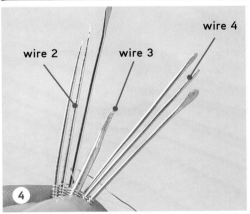

wire 2   wire 3   wire 4

If you are having a hard time compressing the weave right after you add the "V" wire, use the beading awl to get in between the wires and compact the weave.

11 Continue weaving, allowing space to form between Wires 2 and 3 and Wires 3 and 4. Stop weaving when you have created enough space to add a new 20g V-shaped wire, ending on the back of Wire 2, between Wires 2 and 3. Check the back of your work again to make sure you add the new 20g V-shaped wire so it nestles within the last 20g V-shaped wire added.

12 Using the modified soumak weave to create a short wrap row, attach the new "V" wire to the 14g wire (Wire 3) **(Fig. 4)**. Continue weaving, using the basic figure-eight weave, until it's time to add another 20g V-shaped wire. *tip: You will always attach the new 20g V-shaped wire to the 14g wire before continuing with the weave.*

forming the eye of the feather

13 Continue adding 20g V-shaped wires as the space becomes available until you have a total of five. Adjust the angle as needed so that the "V" wires nestle. *note: The angle of each "V" will gradually decrease as you add them into the weave.* After the final 20g V-shaped wire has been added, continue weaving until you reach the hole at the opposite end of the 14g wire. Stop the weave on the right side of the woven base.

The best way to get identical earrings is to make them at the same time. All the base wires should be shaped together and lined up on top of each other to ensure accuracy before beginning weaving.

14 Bend Wires 1–5 farther out from the center. Repeat with Wires 6–10 going in the opposite direction **(Fig. 5)**.

15 Thread one 18g leaf-shaped wire through the hole in the 14g wire, so the point is centered in the hole.

16 Continue to weave with the 30g wire. When you reach the 18g wire, wrap twice around the 18g wire before weaving back across Wires 6–10. *note: Every time you reach the 18g wire, wrap around it twice, except around the curve of the eye. Drop down to one wrap as you weave around this section.*

17 When you reach ¼" (6 mm) from the end of Wire 10, stop and shape Wires 6–10, so they follow the curve of the 18g wire. Continue weaving after you finish shaping the base wires **(Fig. 6)**.

decreasing the weave

18 Begin to decrease the weave about ⅛" (3 mm) from the end of Wire 10.

19 Continue to decrease the weave every three or four rows until just the 18g wire remains. Coil the 30g wire around the 18g wire until it reaches the length of Wire 6. Leave a 4" (10 cm) tail and cut the 30g wire.

weaving the rest of the eye

20 Leaving a 2" (5 cm) tail on the back of the work, coil the 30g wire three times around the left 18g wire. Continue weaving the left side of the earring as you did on the right side **(Fig. 7)**.

21 Weave the two arms of the 18g wires together where they converge just above the tips of the 20g wires, weaving a total of three rows.

22 Cut the 30g wire on the left side 4" (10 cm) from the weave. Wrap this 30g tail wire around the weave between the 18g wires twice, making sure to capture the 30g wire on the right side between the wraps. With the beading awl, lift the wraps in the back to allow room to thread the end of the 30g wire you were wrapping with through the space. After you thread the 30g wire through the space, pull it tight and trim both 30g tail wires. Use flat-nose pliers to gently pinch the space made by the beading awl back into place **(Fig. 8)**.

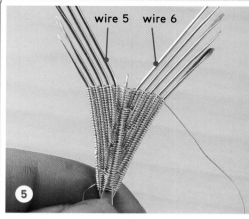

wire 5   wire 6

5

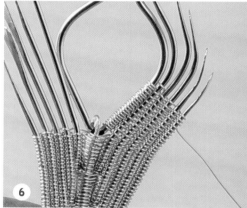

6

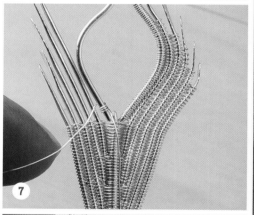

7

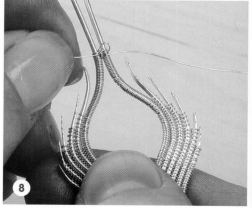

8

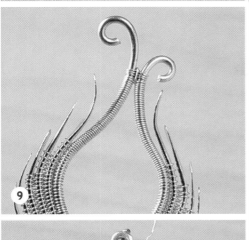

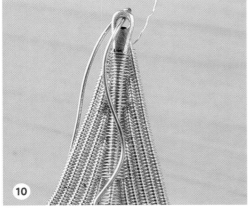

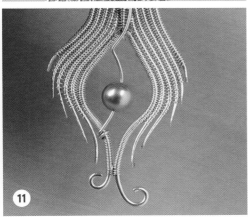

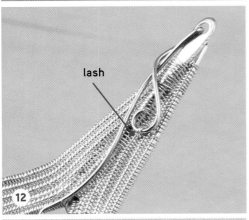

lash

To get the proper spacing and angles, place the second earring on top of the first earring frequently to make sure they match. Be sure to do this before adding each new base wire. Also, when adding the 18g wire to make the eye of the feather, make sure it is a mirror image of the first earring.

weaving the second earring

23 Weave the second earring using the remaining shaped wires and repeat Steps 5–22.

forming the loops

24 Make sure the earrings are identical in size and wire placement and are mirror images in their shaping. Trim the 18g wires to ⅜" (1 cm) and ⅝" (1.5 cm) and then use round-nose pliers to form loops on the end of the wires facing outward. Trim the loops so they are open as shown **(Fig. 9)**.

embellishments

25 Thread the short end of one 22g wire (from Step 4) through the hole at the top of the 14g wire, with the short end of the wire in the back. Using your fingers, bend the longer section of the 22g wire into a loose "S" shape over the front of the earring **(Fig. 10)**.

26 Using flat-nose pliers, gently grasp the 22g wire just below the bottom of the 14g wire, within the eye of the feather. Bend the 22g wire to the right, forming a 90° angle as shown.

27 String one pearl onto the 22g wire and then wrap the 22g wire twice around the 18g wire on the left. Trim the excess 22g wire **(Fig. 11)**. *tip: This step can be done after you have oxidized and polished the earrings to avoid dipping the pearl in the liver of sulfur.*

28 Bring the short end of the 22g wire to the front, creating a gentle "S" shape, and create an organic loop in the wire.

29 Trim the loop so it's open. Use the beading awl to puncture the weave, creating two holes in the weave where the 22g wire ends.

30 Take the 4" (10 cm) 30g wire tail from the beginning of the weave (in Step 6) and thread it from the back of the earring to the front through one of the holes you punctured in the weave. Secure the loop on the 22g wire to the weave by bringing the 30g wire over the 22g wire, down through a hole in the weave, back up through the other hole in the weave, and around the 22g loop a second time. Thread the 30g wire back through a hole in the weave to the back of the earring **(Fig. 12)**.

31 On the back of the earring, use the beading awl to lift up the tip of the "V" on the 20g V-shaped wire nearest the point where the 22g wire was attached **(Fig. 13)**. Wrap the 30g tail wire from Step 30 around the tip of the "V" three times **(Fig. 14)**. Trim the tail wire. Push the tip of the 20g V-shaped wire back down into place with flat-nose pliers.

32 Repeat Steps 25–31 to embellish the second earring, making sure to create a mirror image of the first earring.

finishing touches

33 Using round-nose pliers, bend the ends of the 20g wires back and forth in a few spots to give each tip a wavy or curved shape **(Fig. 15)**.

34 Using your fingers, shape the earring so it looks like a gentle wave from the side **(Fig. 16)**.

35 Repeat Steps 33–34 for the second earring. Attach a French ear wire (see page 41) to the top of each earring.

36 Oxidize the earrings with liver of sulfur and then polish them with steel wool and the brass bristle brush. Use a polishing cloth or a tumbler to clean and brighten the jewelry.

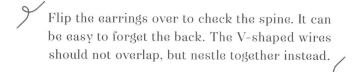

Flip the earrings over to check the spine. It can be easy to forget the back. The V-shaped wires should not overlap, but nestle together instead.

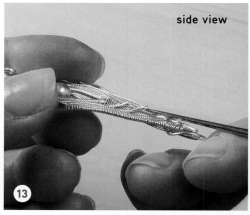

side view

13

back view

14

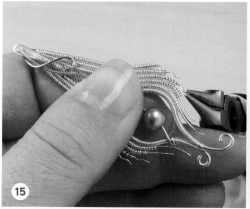

15

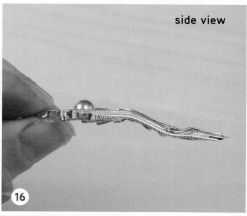

side view

16

MATERIALS

20" (51 cm) of 18g fine silver wire

32" (81.5 cm) of 20g fine silver wire

6" (15 cm) of 24g fine silver wire

20' (6 m) of 28g fine silver wire in a spool or on a bobbin

2 sterling silver rounds, 4mm

2 sterling silver rounds, 3mm

2 padparadscha crystal rounds, 4mm

2" (5 cm) of sterling silver 1.9mm oval chain

1 pair of sterling silver spiral posts (see page 40 for materials and instructions)

1 pair of sterling silver post backs

TOOLS

Ruler

Flush cutters or wire cutters

Fine-point permanent marker

Steel ring-sizing mandrel

Chasing hammer

Steel bench block

Flat-nose pliers

Rawhide mallet

Painter's tape

Round-nose pliers

2mm dowel (optional)

Needle file

Tile

Protective eyewear

Cross-locking tweezers

Butane micro torch

Quenching bowl

Liver of sulfur

#0000 extra-fine steel wool

Soft brass wire bristle brush or toothbrush

Polishing cloth (optional)

Tumbler (optional)

ruffles & lace
CHANDELIER EARRINGS

Create a wonderful lattice design by incorporating rounded ruffles into the weave.

level ⇒ **ADVANCED**

finished length ⇒ 1½" wide x 2¾" long (3.8 x 7 cm)

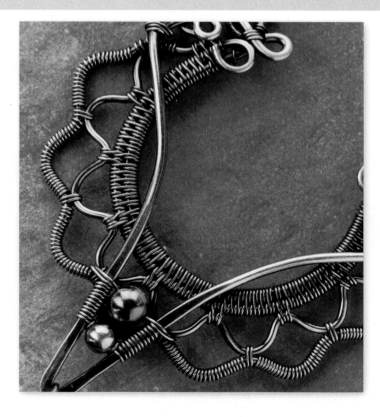

cutting and forming the wires

1 Cut two 4" (10 cm) pieces of 18g wire. Mark the center of each wire with the permanent marker. Form each wire around the ring mandrel at the size 10 mark to create a "U" shape, making sure the "arms" are parallel and with the mark on each wire centered in the curve of the "U." Use the chasing hammer and steel bench block to hammer each wire flat where it curves.

2 Cut two 6" (15 cm) pieces of 18g wire. Mark the center of each wire. Using flat-nose pliers, bend each length of wire at the mark to form a "V" with about a 20° angle. Using your fingers, gently flare out the arms on each of the V-shaped wires starting ¾" (2 cm) up from the point of the "V." Using the chasing hammer and steel bench block, hammer 1" (2.5 cm) of the point on each "V," making sure not to over-flatten the wires **(Fig. 1)**.

3 Cut two 4" (10 cm) pieces of 20g wire. Mark the center of each wire. Form each wire around the ring mandrel at the size 13 mark, creating a "U" shape, making sure the arms are parallel and with the mark on each wire centered in the curve of the "U." Tap the curved sections of each wire with the rawhide mallet on the steel bench block to work-harden. Cut four 7" (18 cm) pieces of 20g wire. Mark each wire 1" (2.5 cm) in from one end.

weaving

4 With the "U" shapes on the bottom, nestle one 18g U-shaped wire from Step 1 inside one 20g U-shaped wire from Step 3 (the 20g wire should be on the outside). It's okay if the center marks do not line up. Line up the marked end of one 7" (18 cm) piece of 20g wire from Step 3 with the left side of the 20g U-shaped wire, so the marked end of the 7" (18 cm) wire is flush with the end of the 20g wire **(Fig. 2)**. Tape all three wires together at the 1" (2.5 cm) mark on the 7" (18 cm) wire as shown. The wires will be referenced by number starting with the innermost wire (the 18g) as Wire 1, followed by Wires 2 and 3.

5 Leaving a 6" (15 cm) tail, use the 28g wire to weave all three wires together using the modified soumak weave, starting at the 1" (2.5 cm) mark. Weave three complete rows, stopping the weave at Wire 1. Push Wire 3 out at a 45° angle to the weave.

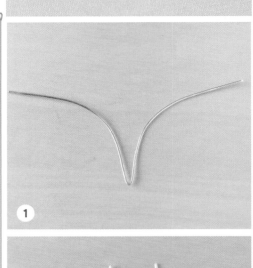

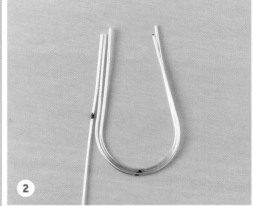

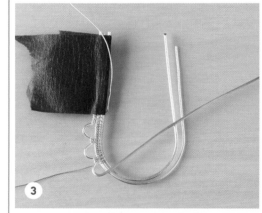

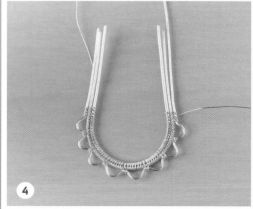

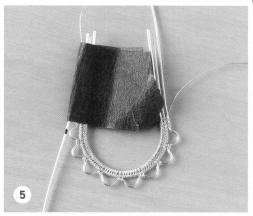

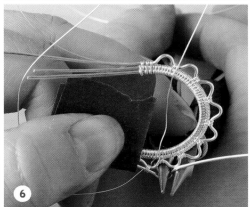

forming the plain ruffles

6   Using round-nose pliers (or a 2mm dowel), form a ruffle in Wire 3. (See How to Create Rounded Ruffles on page 144 for instructions.)

7   Weave Wires 1 and 2 together until just before the point where Wire 3 touches Wire 2; at this point, weave all three wires together for two complete rows.

8   Form another ruffle with the round-nose pliers (or 2mm dowel). Once again weave Wires 1 and 2 together until you are ready to weave in Wire 3 where it begins to touch Wire 2. Weave all three wires together for two complete rows. Continue forming ruffles around the curve and weaving them in where they meet Wire 2 **(Fig. 3)**.

9   There should be a total of eight plain ruffles. At this point, the ruffles might not be centered on the base wire. This will be corrected in Step 19. After finishing the ruffles, weave Wires 1, 2, and 3 together for three rows **(Fig. 4)**. Remove the painter's tape and set aside.

10 Repeat Steps 4–9 to create the second earring, matching it to the first earring.

forming the coiled ruffles

11 Take one 7" (18 cm) piece of 20g wire from Step 3 and line up the 1" (2.5 cm) mark to the center of the first plain ruffle; this will be Wire 4. Tape Wire 4 to the woven form. Measure 4' (122 cm) of 28g wire **(Fig. 5)**.

12 Leaving a 6" (15 cm) tail, use the 28g wire to lash Wires 3 and 4 together three times at the top of the curve on the first plain ruffle on the left.

13 Fit the back of the round-nose pliers between the first two plain ruffles as shown, and then grasp Wire 4 and bend it over the jaw of the pliers to form the first coiled ruffle. Use round-nose pliers to bend Wire 4 to a rounded 90° angle where it intersects the curve of the next plain ruffle **(Fig. 6)**.

14 Coil around Wire 4 until it touches the curve of the plain ruffle; at that point, lash Wires 4 and 3 together twice **(Fig. 7)**.

how to create rounded ruffles

Rounded ruffles are more difficult than pointed ruffles (see instructions on page 31) because you have to make them as you go. Practice making them on scrap wire before continuing with the earrings. Dowels, bail pliers, a beading awl, round-nose pliers, and knitting needles all work great to make rounded ruffles. If you are using a beading awl or round-nose pliers, use painter's tape to mark the position you want to use on the tool.

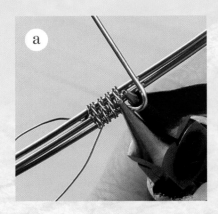

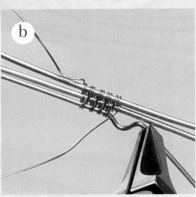

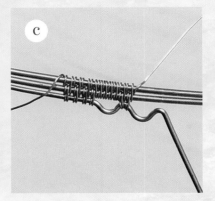

1 Weave the base wires together. Bend the outer base wire at a 45° angle where you want the ruffle to form. Using a round tool in the desired size, gently hold the outer wire at the tip. Bend the wire around the tool so that the wire now crosses over the other base wires **(Fig. A)**.

2 Take the flat-nose pliers and grip the shaped wire at the point where it crosses over the first base wire. Bend the wire at a 45° angle from the rest of the base wires **(Fig. B)**.

3 Continue to weave the base wires together, omitting the shaped ruffle. Start to weave the ruffle into the weave just before the point where the shaped wire touches the base wires. Weave one or two rows. Repeat to create another ruffle **(Fig. C)**.

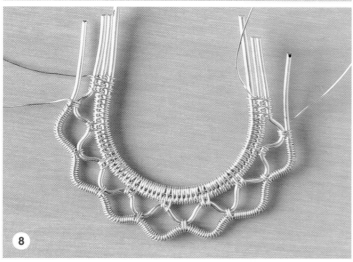

15 Continue making coiled ruffles around the curve, attaching them to the plain ruffles where they touch at the top of the curve. Stop when you have lashed around the last plain ruffle and then lash the last ruffle three times.

16 Repeat Steps 11–15 for the second earring, matching it to the first earring.

trimming and making loops

17 Remove the tape. Mark Wire 4 with the permanent marker ½" (1.3 cm) from the last lashings on both sides of the curve. Mark Wires 2 and 3 at ⅜" (1 cm) from the end of the weave. Mark Wire 1 at ½" (1.3 cm) from the end of the weave. Trim the wires at the marks and file the ends smooth **(Fig. 8)**.

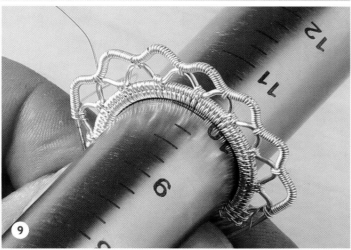

18 Position the woven form on the ring mandrel at the size 10 mark. Re-form the woven section around the mandrel, this time creating a crescent shape rather than a "U" shape. This will make the woven form symmetrical **(Fig. 9)**.

19 Using round-nose pliers, create a small inward loop on the ends of Wire 4, with a slight swirl to it, as shown.

20 Repeat on the ends of Wire 3, except form the loops outward and make the loops larger than those on Wire 4.

21 Repeat Step 20 for the ends of Wire 2, creating small inward loops that sit above those on Wire 4 **(Fig. 10)**.

22 Repeat Steps 17–21 for the second earring.

attaching the v-shaped wires

23 Center one V-shaped wire on the front of the woven form so the point of the "V" is below the center of the ruffles as shown. Tape the point down. Using the 28g wire tail from the end of Wire 4 (on the right), lash the right side of the V-shaped wire three times to the end of Wire 4, just above where the lashings ended on Wire 4. Coil the 28g wire around the first inner ruffle of Wire 3 until you reach the weave, as shown; trim the excess 28g wire on the back of the earring **(Fig. 11)**.

24 With your fingers, curve the end of the V-shaped wire inward. This bend can be more dramatic, crossing over the loops of Wires 2 and 3 as shown, or it can be a gentler curve that frames the loop of Wire 3, as seen in the main photo (page 140). Using the last 28g tail on this side of the earring, lash the V-shaped wire three times to Wire 1.

25 Coil the 28g wire three times around just Wire 1. Trim the excess 28g wire on the back of the earring. With the round-nose pliers, form a loop on the end of Wire 1 going outward, using the full length of the exposed wire to form the loop. Mark the end of the V-shaped wire ¼" (6 mm) from where it is coiled to Wire 1. Trim the wire at the mark and file the ends smooth **(Fig. 12)**. Using round-nose pliers, form a simple loop on the end of the V-shaped wire, facing outward and sitting above the loop on Wire 2 as shown **(Fig. 13)**.

26 Secure the left side of the V-shaped wire, making sure it mirrors the right side.

27 Repeat Steps 23–26 for the second earring.

back view

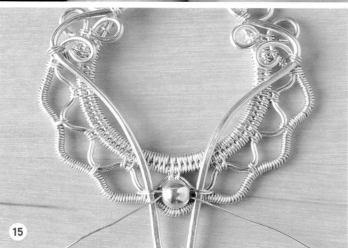

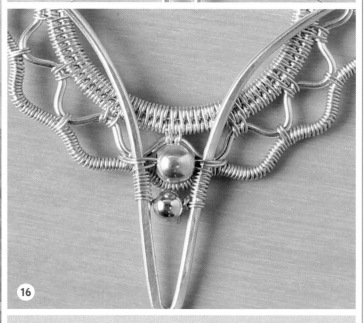

securing the "v" tip

28 Remove the tape. Using your fingers, compress the "V" at the center of the woven form. This will exaggerate the wire flaring out from the point **(Fig. 14)**.

29 Cut 12" (30.5 cm) of 28g wire. String one sterling silver 4mm round onto the 28g wire and push it to the center of the wire. Position the round over the "V" where it intersects the plain ruffle as shown. Use the 28g wire to secure the "V" wire by lashing each side of the "V" to the woven form. You will be lashing the 28g wire twice around the existing lashes that connect the two ruffles together and the new lashes will be perpendicular to the existing lashes.

30 Wrap once around each side of the "V" with the 28g wire before threading the 28g wire back through the 4mm round **(Fig. 15)**. Coil the 28g wires down each side of the "V" six times. String one 3mm round onto one 28g wire and bring the wire over to the opposite side of the "V." Thread the second 28g wire through the round and over to the opposite side of the "V" **(Fig. 16)**. *tip: The 28g wires will be crisscrossing through the center of the round.* Wrap each 28g wire once around the arm of the "V." Wrap each wire twice around the wire passing through the center of the 3mm round. Trim the excess 28g wire on the back of the earring **(Fig. 17)**.

31 Repeat Steps 28–30 for the second earring.

finishing touches

32 Cut two 3" (7.5 cm) pieces of 24g wire. Place the tile on your work surface and put on the protective eyewear. Holding the wire with cross-locking tweezers, use the micro torch to ball one end of each wire to create two head pins. Quench.

33. String one crystal round onto one head pin and begin a wrapped loop, capturing the "V" tip inside the loop before completing the wrap. Trim the excess wire.

34 Cut the chain into four ½" (1.3 cm) pieces. *tip: If you change the type of chain, make sure the links are large enough to slip over the 18g wire.* Attach the earring post to the last link on two of the ½" (1.3 cm) chains Using flat-nose pliers, gently "twist" the loops on Wire 1 open (as you would a jump ring) and slip the chain onto the wire so the ear post is oriented correctly. If necessary, remove a chain link on both sides to help orientate the earrings. Gently twist the loops back into position to close.

35 Repeat Steps 33–34 for the second earring.

36 Oxidize both earrings with liver of sulfur and polish with the steel wool and brass brush. Use a polishing cloth or a tumbler to clean and polish the jewelry.

I normally like to start in the center when working with curves. It is easier to weave and easier to get a symmetrical design. However, rounded curves need to be made by starting on one side and going around. I hold the weave to the side; this makes it easier to bring the 28g wire around the curve.

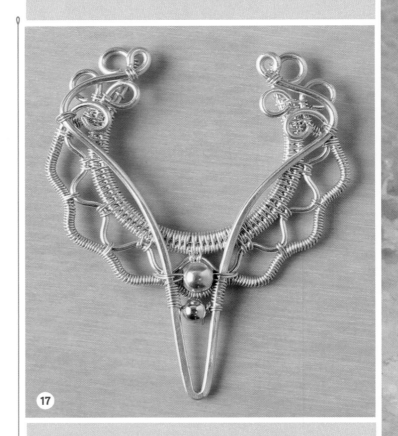

17

variation

Create this necklace with copper wire and a large, round green lampwork bead in the center, adjusting the curvature to fit the bead. Add matching drops to the ruffles for more splashes of color. Mix the ruffles up with pointed inner ruffles and rounded outer ruffles or change the size of the ruffles. (See page 31 for instructions on making pointed ruffles.)

TECHNIQUES

Modified Soumak Weave (page 24)

Loops (page 27)

Lashing (page 18)

Forming (page 21)

Hammering (page 32)

Embellishing (page 35)

MATERIALS

3½" (9 cm) of 16g fine silver wire

27" (68.5 cm) of 18g fine silver wire

8" (20.5 cm) of 22g fine silver wire

4" (10 cm) of 26g fine silver wire

12' (3.6 m) of 28g fine silver wire

1 sterling silver round, 4mm

1 sterling silver round, 2mm

5 sterling silver rounds, 3mm

1 mint green pearl, 5mm

16" (40.5 cm) of sterling silver 1mm oval chain

Simple S-clasp (see page 43 for materials and instructions)

TOOLS

Ruler

Flush cutters or wire cutters

Fine-point permanent marker

Round-nose pliers

Needle file

Chasing hammer

Steel bench block

Painter's tape

7mm dowel (or round #2 pencil)

Steel ring-sizing mandrel (optional)

Chain-nose pliers

Liver of sulfur

#0000 extra-fine steel wool

Soft brass wire bristle brush or toothbrush

Polishing cloth (optional)

Tumbler (optional)

calligraphy
PENDANT

Swirl and twirl the base wires as you weave them together, creating a seamless flowing design from start to finish.

level ⇒ **ADVANCED**

finished size ⇒ 3" wide x 1½" high (7.5 x 3.8 cm)

length ⇒ 21" (53.5 cm)

cutting and forming the wire

1   Cut 3½" (9 cm) of 16g wire and mark the center of the wire with the permanent marker; this is Wire 1. Use round-nose pliers to create an open loop on one end of the wire and then loosely spiral the wire around the loop for a half turn. *tip: Because you'll be using a lot of force to create the loop with the heavy wire, you'll create ugly tool marks. Trim the tip of the loop to remove these marks.* Using your fingers, curve the middle of the wire. Use round-nose pliers to bend the opposite end of the wire so it curves back slightly toward the looped end; this is the tail. Trim the tail if needed to remove the tool marks and file the end flat. Use the chasing hammer and steel bench block to flare out the looped end and create a paddle on the tail end as shown. Round the paddle with the file **(Fig. 1)**.

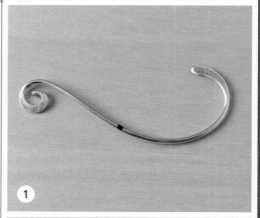

2   Cut 9" (23 cm) of 18g wire and mark it 3½" (9 cm) in from one end; this is Wire 2. Place Wire 2 on top of Wire 1, with the 3½" (9 cm) length on the left. Line up the mark on Wire 2 with the top of the spiral on Wire 1. Using your fingers, bend Wire 2 so it follows the curve of Wire 1 **(Fig. 2)**. Tape both wires together at the center mark on Wire 1, leaving the left half exposed.

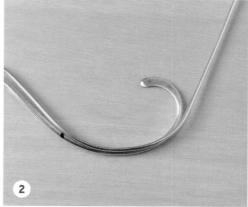

3   Use the 7mm dowel to create a large loop in Wire 2 next to the spiral on Wire 1, ending with Wire 2 on the back. Organically loop Wire 2 inward near the center mark on Wire 1, with the Wire 2 loop facing Wire 2. Trim the loop **(Fig. 3)**.

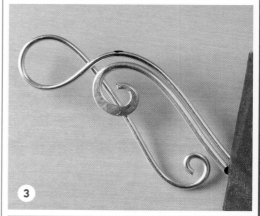

4   Cut 7" (18 cm) of 18g wire; this is Wire 3. Using round-nose pliers, create an open loop on one end and then loosely spiral the wire around the loop for a half turn. Place the spiraled end of Wire 3 on top of the large loop on Wire 2, with the spiral facing outward. Using your fingers, bend Wire 3 so it follows the same curved path as Wire 2. Place Wire 3 on the steel bench block and use the chasing hammer to flare out the spiral **(Fig. 4)**.

5   Cut 5" (12.5 cm) of 18g wire; this is Wire 4. Using round-nose pliers, create an open loop and then loosely spiral the wire around the loop for one turn. Use the chasing hammer to flare out the swirl as before. Set aside.

6   Cut 6" (15 cm) of 18g wire and repeat Step 5 to create the loop, spiral, and then flare out the swirl. Set aside.

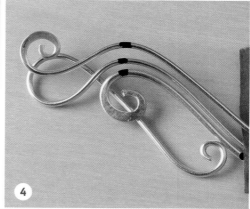

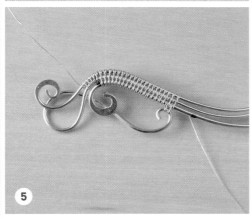

5

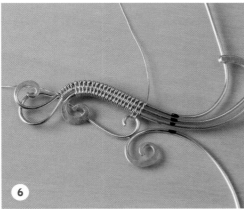

6

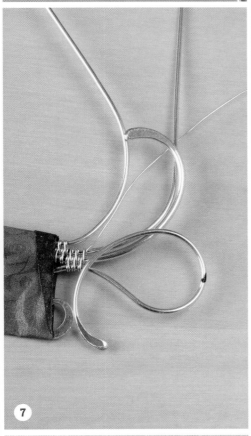

7

Halfway through the weave you will be threading the 28g wire through an enclosed area, so you won't be able to use a bobbin to help keep the wire from tangling in this project.

weaving

7 Use the permanent marker to mark Wire 1 and 3 where they touch the mark on Wire 2. Remove the tape. Fit Wires 2 and 3 together with Wire 3 above. Push the back end of Wire 2 out of the way to give you room to weave. Leaving a 6" (15 cm) tail, use the 28g wire to weave Wires 2 and 3 together using the modified soumak weave, starting with Wire 3, and just to the left of where the large loop on Wire 2 crosses over itself. Weave to the mark on Wire 2.

8 Place Wire 1 below Wire 2, lining up the two marks. Weave all three wires together until you come to the point where the organic loop on Wire 2 touches Wire 1. Wrap twice around the open loop on Wire 2 to secure it to Wire 1. Continue weaving Wires 1, 2, and 3 for one row. Thread the 28g wire back through the organic loop on Wire 2 to secure it to Wire 1 for a second time **(Fig. 5)**.

9 Place Wire 4 below Wire 1, with the swirl facing downward and sitting below the organic loop on Wire 2. Mark all four wires where Wire 4 touches Wire 1 **(Fig. 6)**. Continue weaving Wires 1, 2, and 3 together until you reach the marks. Tape Wire 4 to the woven base to secure it as you weave.

10 Weave Wires 4, 1, and 2 together for three rows. Mark Wire 4 at 1" (2.5 cm) from the weave. Using your fingers, bend the end of Wire 4 up and around into a loop with the 1" (2.5 cm) mark in the center of the loop. *tip: This loop can also be made using the tip of the ring mandrel.*

11 Using round-nose pliers, curve the Wire 4 tail so it sits next to the swirl of Wire 4 (the swirl is sticking out slightly from under the tape). Curve the tail a bit more and then trim the excess wire below the swirl of Wire 4. Push the Wire 4 tail out of the way and place it on the steel bench block. Use the chasing hammer to create a paddle on the end of the wire. Round the end with the file. Reposition the tail and remove the tape **(Fig. 7)**.

12 Mark Wire 3 at ½" (1.3 cm) from the weave. Using your fingers, loop the wire around and behind the woven form, with the mark in the center of the loop. Weave Wires 1 and 2 and the tail end of Wire 4 together for two rows. Decrease to Wires 1 and 2. Weave together for a few rows and stop weaving when you come to the point where the loops of Wire 3 and 4 would touch if you pinched them together. This should be right above Wire 2 (**Fig. 8**).

13 After wrapping around Wire 2, thread the 28g wire through the two loops and lash Wires 3 and 4 together twice. Bring the 28g wire around to the back and weave Wires 1 and 2 together for one row. Thread the 28g wire through the two loops again and wrap around Wires 3 and 4 once.

14 Finish weaving Wires 1 and 2 together, stopping the weave just beyond the end of the loop on Wire 4 and with enough room between Wires 1 and 4 to fit the 4mm round. String the 4mm round onto the 28g wire to test the fit between the wires and then remove it.

Because the base wires are preshaped, you will need to be careful as you weave not to bend them out of shape.

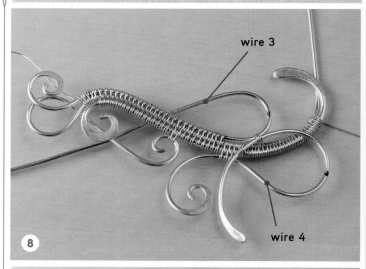

wire 3

wire 4

8

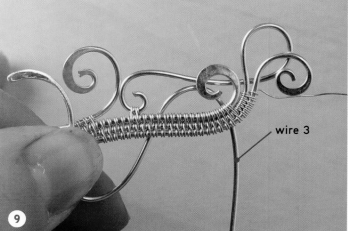

wire 3

9

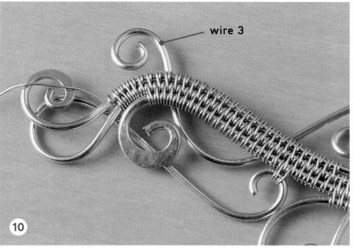

wire 3

10

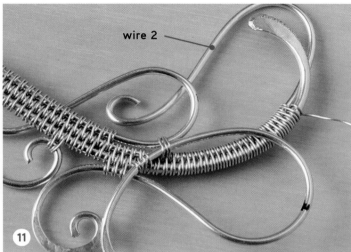

wire 2

11

forming

15 Hold the woven form upside down with Wire 3 in the back of the weave. Using your fingers, curve Wire 3 up into an arc that sits between the organic loop on Wire 2 and below the spiral on Wire 1 as shown and behind the weave again **(Fig. 9)**. Organically loop Wire 3 to create a loop in the end of the wire. Trim the loop as shown, ending with an open loop **(Fig. 10)**.

16 On the opposite end of the woven form, use your fingers to bend Wire 2 up and around into a large loop extending beyond Wire 1. Bring the wire back down behind the large loop of Wire 3. Organically loop Wire 2 to create a loop inside the loop of Wire 3. Trim the Wire 2 loop so you end up with an open loop as shown **(Fig. 11)**.

17 Place Wire 5 at the back of the woven form, with the swirl on the right, facing up and inward, between Wires 2 and 4. Wire 5 needs to touch Wire 4 where you will be adding the 4mm round. Tape Wire 5 to the woven form.

18 String one 4mm round onto the 28g wire at the end of Wire 1. Bring the 28g wire over to Wire 4 and lash Wires 4 and 5 together three times before passing the 28g wire back through the 4mm round. Mark where Wires 2 and 5 touch (as seen in **Fig. 12**). Coil the 28g wire around Wire 2 until you reach the mark. Lash Wires 2 and 5 together three times. Continue coiling Wire 2 until you have enough space to add the 2mm round between Wires 2 and 5.

19 String the 2mm round onto the 28g wire and bring the wire over to Wire 5. Wrap twice around Wire 5 before passing the 28g wire back through the round. Finish coiling the length of Wire 2, stopping when you reach the open loop at the end.

20 Remove the tape. Lash Wires 2 and 5 together three times. *tip: Wires 2 and 5 should be sitting above and behind the woven form.* Thread the 28g wire through the lashings just made and wrap around the lashing; trim the excess wire **(Fig. 12)**. Using your fingers, bend Wire 5 over to the front of the weave and form into a gentle arc that touches the outside swirl on Wire 1. Bring Wire 5 up behind the large loop on Wire 2. Organically loop Wire 5 to create a loop above the weave and between the simple loops on each end of Wire 3. *note: This loop needs to be large enough for one 3mm round to fit inside.*

21 Trim the loop on Wire 5 to create an open loop **(Fig. 13)**. String one 3mm round onto the 28g wire around Wire 3. Bring the wire behind the bottom of the simple loop on Wire 5 and then over the opposite side of the same loop. Lash Wires 3 and 5 together three times before passing the 28g wire back through the round. Wrap the 28g wire around Wire 3 once before wrapping it twice around the wires passing through the round. Trim the excess 28g wire **(Fig. 14)**.

22 Oxidize the pendant, remaining silver rounds, 26g wire, 22g wire, and chain with liver of sulfur. Polish with the steel wool and brass brush. Use a polishing cloth or tumbler to clean and brighten the pendant.

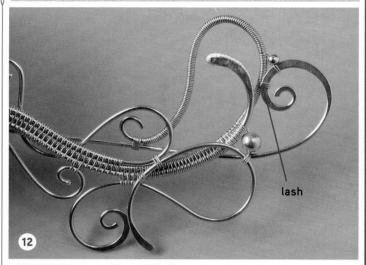

12 lash

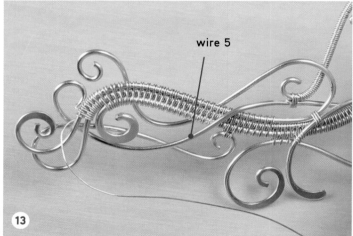

wire 5

13

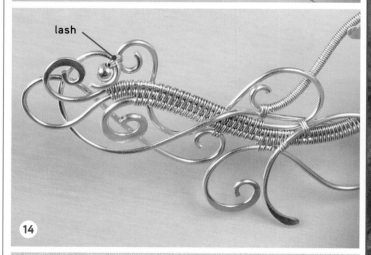

lash

14

final embellishments

23 Center the 5mm pearl on the 4" (10 cm) piece of 26g wire. Hold the pearl in place on the left side of the pendant, between the swirls on Wires 2 and 4. Wrap each side of the 26g wire twice around Wires 2 and 4 and then wrap twice around the wire, passing through the pearl on each side. Trim the excess wire.

24 Using your fingers, curve the pendant in an alternating wave pattern to give it more dimension.

25 Cut the chain in half. Cut four 2" (5 cm) pieces of 22g wire. Using round-nose pliers, begin a wrapped loop on one end of each wire. Attach one loop to each of the four chain ends; complete the wrap. String one 3mm silver round onto each wire and begin a second wrapped loop on each wire, with two of these loops being large enough for the clasp to fit through. Attach a smaller loop to each side of the pendant; complete each wrap. Attach a larger loop to the S-clasp; complete the wrap. Complete the wrap on the second larger loop. Hook the S-clasp into this loop to close the necklace. Polish the completed necklace.

variation

For this copper version, use copper wire, copper rounds, and a faceted brown glass rondelle.

TECHNIQUES

Modified Soumak Weave (page 24)

Lashing Weave (page 26)

Forming (page 21)

Lashing (page 18)

Loops (page 27)

Hammering (page 32)

Annealing (page 20)

Beveling Flattened Wire (page 33)

Embellishing (page 35)

Folding Hammered Wire (page 30)

Symmetry (page 34)

MATERIALS

10" (25.5 cm) of 18g fine silver wire

7¾" (19.5 cm) of 20g fine silver wire

8½' (5.6 m) of 28g fine silver wire

22" (56 cm) of 24g fine silver wire

5 sterling silver rounds, 2mm

4 sterling silver rounds, 3mm

1 sterling silver round, 4mm

5 peridot AB crystal bicones, 2x4mm

1 aquamarine Sahara Baroque crystal pendant, 16mm

16" (40.5 cm) of sterling silver 2.5mm oval chain

Decorative S-clasp (see page 43 for materials and instructions)

TOOLS

Ruler

Flush cutters or wire cutters

Fine-point permanent marker

Steel ring-sizing mandrel

Steel bench block

Rawhide mallet

Needle file

Round-nose pliers

Chasing hammer

Painter's tape

Flat-nose pliers

Charcoal block

Protective eyewear

Cross-locking tweezers

Butane micro torch

Quenching bowl

Liver of sulfur

#0000 extra-fine steel wool

Soft brass wire bristle brush or toothbrush

Polishing cloth (optional)

Tumbler (optional)

kayla
PENDANT

Learn how to make smaller components and layer them to make a seamless and intricate design.

level ⇒ **ADVANCED**

finished size ⇒ 1½" wide x 2⅛" high (3.8 x 5.3 cm)

length ⇒ 16" (40.5 cm)

creating the woven frame
(component 1)

1 Cut 1¾" (4.5 cm) of 20g wire and mark the center with the permanent marker. Center the mark at size 5 on the ring mandrel and bend the wire around the mandrel. Tap the shaped wire on the bench block with the rawhide mallet. This is Wire 1.

2 Cut 2" (5 cm) of 18g wire and mark the center of the wire. File the ends flat. Using the tip of the round-nose pliers, make identical-sized simple loops on each end of the wire, with the loops facing inward toward each other. Mark each end of the wire ¼" (6 mm) in from the loop. Center the wire at size 8 on the ring mandrel with the loops facing outward, then form the wire around the mandrel. Use the chasing hammer and steel bench block to lightly flatten the wire and the loops. Re-mark the center line. This is Wire 2.

3 Place Wire 1 inside Wire 2 and line up the center marks. Tape the wires together so the tape covers the left half.

4 Cut 3' (91.5 cm) of 28g wire. Starting in the center of the 28g wire, weave Wires 1 and 2 together from the center mark, weaving to the ¼" (6 mm) mark on Wire 2.

5 Remove the tape. Weave the other half of Wires 1 and 2 with the remaining 28g wire, stopping at the ¼" (6 mm) mark on this side of Wire 2 **(Fig. 1)**.

creating the outer "V" shapes
(component 2)

6 Cut 6" (15 cm) of 18g wire and mark the center of the wire. Using flat-nose pliers, make a 90° bend at the mark, creating a "V" shape. This is Wire 3.

7 Cut 6" (15 cm) of 20g wire and mark the center of the wire. Using flat-nose pliers, make a 20° bend at the mark, creating a "V" shape. Grasp the inside tip of the "V" with the flat-nose pliers and bend the

left "arm" outward at the edge of the pliers; repeat on the right side. The arms should form a 90° angle. This is Wire 4 **(Fig. 2)**.

8 Place Wire 3 inside Wire 4, making sure the points line up, then tape the left arms together.

9 Cut 3' (91.5 cm) of 28g wire. Starting at the center of the 28g wire, coil around Wire 4 four times where Wires 3 and 4 meet at the bend. Lash Wires 3 and 4 together twice. Coil Wire 4 six times and then lash Wires 3 and 4 together another two times; repeat for a total of four lashed sections.

10 Bend Wire 4 out to allow room to add one 2mm round. Coil around Wire 4 ten times. String one 2mm round onto the 28g wire. Bring the 28g wire over to Wire 3 and wrap twice around Wire 3 to secure the round, adjusting the angle of Wire 3 so the round fits between Wires 3 and 4. Thread the 28g wire back through the round after securing it to Wire 3 and coil around Wire 4 twelve times.

11 String one 3mm round onto the 28g wire and secure it to Wire 3 as before. Thread the 28g wire back through the round and coil around Wire 4 fourteen times **(Fig. 3)**.

12 Remove the tape. String one 2mm round onto the remaining half of the 28g wire. Bring the 28g wire over to the other arm of Wire 4, with the round sitting between the "Vs" and coil around Wire 4 four times. Lash Wires 3 and 4 twice, then finish this side in the same manner as the first. *note: It is easier if you flip the woven piece so that the "V" is at the top.* **(Fig. 4)**.

13 Position the "V" component so it is facing down and the 2mm bead is in front. Bend the arms of Wire 3 up just above the point where the 28g wire going through the 3mm round is wrapped around Wire 3. Measure the length of each arm first to guarantee that the wrappings holding the 3mm round in place are the same distance from the center, the point of the "V" of Wire 3 **(Fig. 5)**. *tip: For me, this distance is ¾" (2 cm), and that is where I make my bend.*

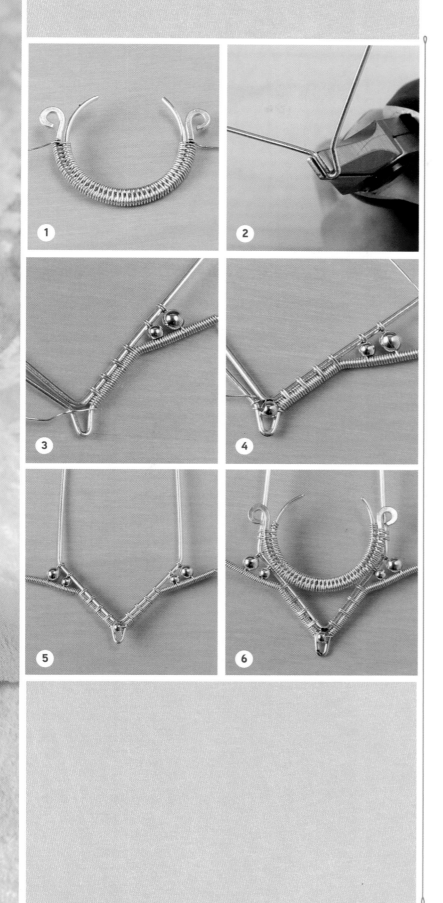

connecting components 1 and 2

14 Place Component 1 inside Component 2. Adjust the angle of Component 2 as needed so the components fit together. *tip: As you add each component, make sure everything lines up down the center before securing the pieces together. With the pointed tips it will be easy to tell that the symmetry is off.* The arms of Wire 3 should be going up and parallel to each other and running along the outside of Wire 2. Using the 28g wire from Component 1, weave Wires 1, 2, and 3 on the right side together for two complete rows using the modified soumak weave. Coil the 28g wire around Wire 1 twice and cut the 28g wire flush. Connect the other side in the same manner **(Fig. 6)**.

15 Trim the ends of Wire 3 to 1½" (3.8 cm) from the end of the weave. Fit the back of the round-nose pliers between the loop of Wire 2 and the 3mm round. Shape Wire 3 down and around the pliers. Continue to curve the arm around in a wide arc to bring the end of the wire up and along the center of the design. *tip: If you're new to making large organic loops, you'll find it easier to create identical loops using round-nose pliers. Once you have some experience, you may be able to make them without tools.* Repeat on the other side. The two arms should come up next to each other in the center of the woven form and the ends should line up. If the ends do not, the wires are not symmetrical. Make the needed adjustments so that they are.

16 On the right side, push Wire 4 over against the loop on Wire 3. Using the 28g wire, lash Wires 3 and 4 together three times at the loop as shown. Coil Wire 3 seven times, then string one 2mm round onto the 28g wire.

17 Bring the 28g wire over to the loop on Wire 2 and wrap twice around the loop to secure the round, then thread the 28g wire back through the 2mm round. Wrap the 28g wire once around Wire 3, then wrap the 28g wire twice around the wire passing through the round **(Fig. 7)**.

18 Trim Wire 4 to 1¼" (3.2 cm) from the top coils. File the ends flat.

19. At the point where Wires 3 and 4 are lashed together, use your fingers to bend Wire 4 down over the front of Wire 3, across the weave, then around and behind Wire 3. Create a loose spiral around Wire 3. Use the tip of the round-nose pliers to create a tiny loop at the end of Wire 4. Push the spiral up against the inner wall of the weave **(Fig. 8)**.

20 Straighten Wire 1 and trim both ends to the same length. Using round-nose pliers, create a simple loop inward **(Fig. 9)**.

21 Repeat Steps 16–20, creating a mirror image on the left side of the pendant.

creating the hammered "V" *(component 3)*

22 Cut 2" (5 cm) of 18g wire and mark the center. Using flat-nose pliers, bend the wire to a 45° angle at the mark, creating a "V." Trim the arms to the same length. Use the chasing hammer and steel bench block to flatten ½" (1.3 cm) of the point. Using the permanent marker, place a line half-way down the jaws of the round-nose pliers. Create identical loops on each end of the wire using the mark on the round-nose pliers as a guide. You want the loops to be 2mm wide. The finished "V" should be ¾" (2 cm) in length.

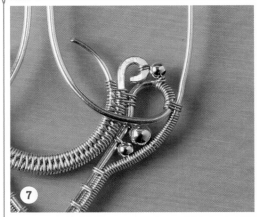

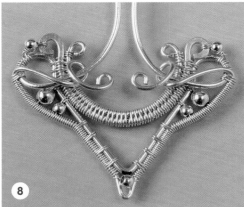

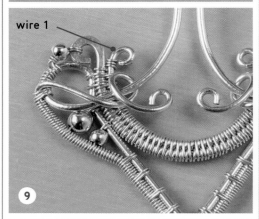

wire 1

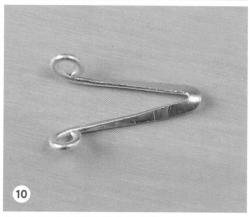

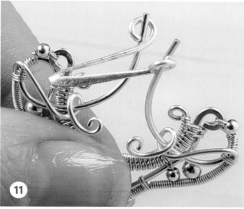

23 Place the charcoal block on your work surface and put on the protective eyewear. Holding the wire with cross-locking tweezers, use the micro torch to anneal the "V." Using flat-nose pliers, and with the loops facing up, grasp one arm of the "V" and fold it at the point; repeat on the other arm. (See page 30 for instructions on folding hammered wire.) Bevel the edges with the file **(Fig. 10)**. *tip: The loops should be rotated out more to the side now. If they're not, use the flat-nose pliers to pivot the loops out at an angle.*

24 Split the two arms of Wire 3 apart, like you would a split ring, with one arm pushed to the back and the other arm pushed to the front. Slip the "V" onto the open ends of Wire 3, with the arms of Wire 3 going through the loop from the outside of the "V" **(Fig. 11)**.

25 Open up each arm of the angle of the "V" with the flat-nose pliers until the loops of the "V" sit against the spiral of Wire 4. Loop the ends of Wire 3, looping out from the center so that the ends are symmetrical and the loops are touching.

26 Cut 18" (45.5 cm) of 28g wire. Grasp each loop on Wire 3 with flat-nose pliers and gently twist it open, as you would a jump ring. Starting in the center of the 28g wire, lash the loops on Wire 3 together where they touch three times.

27 Use the bottom 28g tail wire to coil down the right arm of Wire 3, up to the loop on the right side of the "V" (Component 3). String one 3mm round onto the 28g wire. Bring the 28g wire over to the loop on Wire 1 and wrap twice around the loop, securing the round between the loop and Wire 3. Thread the 28g wire back through the round and wrap once around Wire 3. Wrap the wire twice around the wires passing through the round; trim the excess wire **(Fig. 12)**.

28 Thread the remaining 28g wire tail wire through the back of the lashings between the two arms of Wire 3. Coil the 28g wire around the left arm of Wire 3 and add one 3mm round, as you did on the opposite side, making sure the coils on both sides of Wire 3 are symmetrical in length. Close the loops on Wire 3.

If at any time you are finding that the added metal beads are not fitting the space, change the bead size to larger or smaller.

29 Cut 6" (15 cm) of 28g wire and thread one 4mm round onto the center of the wire. Place the round between the loops on Wire 4 and wrap each side of the 28g wire around the loops twice. Thread each 28g wire tail back through the round and wrap around the loops once. Wrap each tail wire twice around the wires passing through the round; trim the excess wire (**Fig. 13**).

30 Using your fingers, mold the hammered tip of the "V" on Component 3 over the woven frame of Component 1, giving the "V" component a convex curvature or bend. This can be better seen in the finished necklace on page 158. Then curve the back of Component 1 to give it a gentle dome in the front (**Fig. 14**).

finishing touches

31 Cut 4" (10 cm) of 28g wire and string one crystal bicone onto the wire. Wrap each side of the 28g wire twice around the top of the looped ends on Wire 3. Thread each 28g wire tail back through the crystal and wrap once around the loops. Wrap each 28g wire tail twice around the wires passing through the crystal; trim the excess wire.

As you work, the form needs to be flat. At the very end we will hand-form the shape to give it more depth.

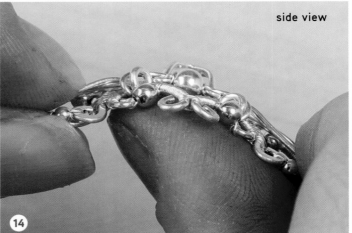

side view

32 Cut 12" (30.5 cm) of 24g wire and string the Baroque crystal pendant onto the wire, with 2" (5 cm) of wire on one side of the pendant hole and 10" (25.5 cm) on the other side. Form a briolette wrapped loop by bringing both sides of the wire together, crossing them at the top of the pendant, and forming a triangle. Straighten the wires so they are parallel. Wrap the short wire around the long wire twice. Trim the short wire flush. Using round-nose pliers, begin a wrapped loop on the long wire, just above the wraps. Slip the loop onto the point of the bottom "V" on the woven pendant and complete the wrapped loop, covering the hole on the crystal pendant. Wrap down the top of the crystal pendant and then cross the wire up over the wraps and back up to the top. Trim the wire near the loop at the top of the crystal pendant and tuck in the cut end.

33 Cut the chain into two 8" (20.5 cm) lengths. Cut four 2" (5 cm) pieces of 24g wire. Begin a wrapped loop on one end of each wire. String one bicone crystal onto each wire and begin a second wrapped loop on the other end. Slip one loop on each link onto the four chain ends; wrap those loops closed. Slip the open loop on two links onto the loops on Wire 2; wrap those loops closed. Slip the open loop on one remaining link onto the bottom of the decorative S-clasp; wrap this loop closed. Wrap the loop on the final link closed. Cut 2" (5 cm) of 24g wire and begin a wrapped loop on one end. Slide this loop onto the end loop of the final bicone link added; wrap this loop closed. String one 3mm silver round onto the wire and create a second wrapped loop that is large enough to attach to the hook on the decorative S-clasp; wrap this loop closed. Use the chasing hammer and steel bench block to flatten the loop.

34 Oxidize the necklace in liver of sulfur and polish with the steel wool and brass brush. Use a polishing cloth or a tumbler to clean and polish the jewelry.

variation

Combine the Danika Post Earrings (page 94) and the Kayla Pendant in copper to form dramatic earrings.

MATERIALS

22½" (57 cm) of 16g sterling silver wire

27" (68.5 cm) of 18g fine silver wire

3" (7.5 cm) of 24g fine silver wire

28" (71 cm) of 26g fine silver wire

12' (3.6 m) of 28g fine silver wire

7 white pearls, 5mm

1" (2.5 cm) of sterling silver 1x3mm flat oval chain

TOOLS

Ruler

Flush cutters or wire cutters

Needle file

Fine-point permanent marker

7mm dowel (or round #2 pencil)

4mm dowel (or back of the round-nose pliers)

Round-nose pliers

Chasing hammer

Steel bench block

Charcoal block or fire brick

Cross-locking tweezers

Protective eyewear

Butane micro torch

Quenching bowl

Pickling solution (optional)

Painter's tape

Beading awl

Flat-nose pliers

Steel ring-sizing mandrel (optional)

Liver of sulfur

#0000 extra-fine steel wool

Soft brass wire bristle brush or toothbrush

Tumbler (optional)

Polishing cloth (optional)

elandra
BRACELET

Elandra was inspired by the decorative S-clasp (page 43). I'd been trying to create a link-based design when it occurred to me that the S-clasp would make a pretty link. Sometimes we get so hung up on doing things one way that we fail to see what's right in front of us the whole time.

level ⟹ **ADVANCED**

length ⟹ 6¼" (16 cm), adjusts to 7" (18 cm)

cutting and forming the wire

1 Cut six 3¾" (9.5 cm) pieces of 16g wire. File one end on each wire flat. Starting at the filed end, mark each wire at 1" (2.5 cm), 2" (5 cm), and 3" (7.5 cm) with the permanent marker. Bend each wire around the 7mm dowel at the 1" (2.5 cm) mark, creating a "U" shape, centering the 1" (2.5 cm) mark in the curve of the "U." Use the back of the round-nose pliers or a 4mm dowel to bend the wire in the opposite direction at the 2" (5 cm) mark, with the 2" (5 cm) mark centered in the curve. Using round-nose pliers, bend the filed end outward to create a tail **(Fig. 1)**. Use the chasing hammer and steel bench block to create a paddle on the tail. Hammer the curved sections and the wire past the 3" (7.5 cm) mark to flatten. Round each of the tails with the file **(Fig. 2)**. Place the charcoal block or fire brick on your work surface or hold the wire with cross-locking tweezers; put on the protective eyewear. Use the micro torch to anneal all six wires. Quench. *note: If you're using sterling silver or copper, pickle the wires according to the manufacturer's directions.*

2 Cut six 4½" (11.5 cm) pieces of 18g wire. Using the micro torch, form a small ball on one end of each wire. Trim the wires to 4" (10 cm). Ball the trimmed ends, making this ball slightly larger than the one on the other end. Each finished wire should be 3¾" (9.5 cm).

weaving

3 Place one 16g wire on the ruler with the large U-shaped curve on the left and the tail at the bottom. Re-mark the center line in the large "U" (the 1" [2.5 cm] mark). Mark the "middle arm" ⅝" (1.5 cm) from the 1" (2.5 cm) mark.

4 Mark one 18g wire 2" (5 cm) in from the smaller balled end. Place the 18g wire on top of the 16g wire, aligning the 2" (5 cm) mark with the 1" (2.5 cm) mark on the 16g wire, with the smaller balled end above. Bend the 18g wire so it follows the shape of the middle arm of the 16g wire, bringing it down behind the smaller "U" shape. *tip: Tape the bottom of the 18g wire to the 16g tail wire to secure the wires before beginning the weave.* Cut 2' (61 cm) of 28g wire.

5 Leaving a 6" (15 cm) tail, use the 28g wire to weave the 18g and 16g wires together using the modified soumak weave, beginning at the 1" (2.5 cm) mark and ending at the ⅝" (1.5 cm) mark. Remove the tape and push the 16g tail over so it intersects the middle arm at the ⅝" (1.5 cm) mark; lash the tail to the middle arm three times **(Fig. 3)**.

6 Thread the 28g wire through the space between the lashings and wrap twice around the lashings to secure the 28g wire. *tip: If you're having difficulty threading the 28g wire through the lashings a second time, use the beading awl to make room in the lashings for the wire to pass through.* Trim the excess 28g wire.

attaching links

7 Push the 18g wire up at the ⅝" (1.5 cm) mark. Thread the chain onto the "upper arm" of the 16g wire and slide it down into the smaller U-shaped curve **(Fig. 4)**.

8 Bring the upper arm behind the weave, intersecting near the ⅝" (1.5 cm) mark. Flip the woven form over and curve the 16g wire arm as shown, ending with the tail bending upward at the right and crossing over the 1" (2.5 cm) mark.

9 Using flat-nose pliers, bend the tail perpendicular to the large U-shaped curve **(Fig. 5)**.

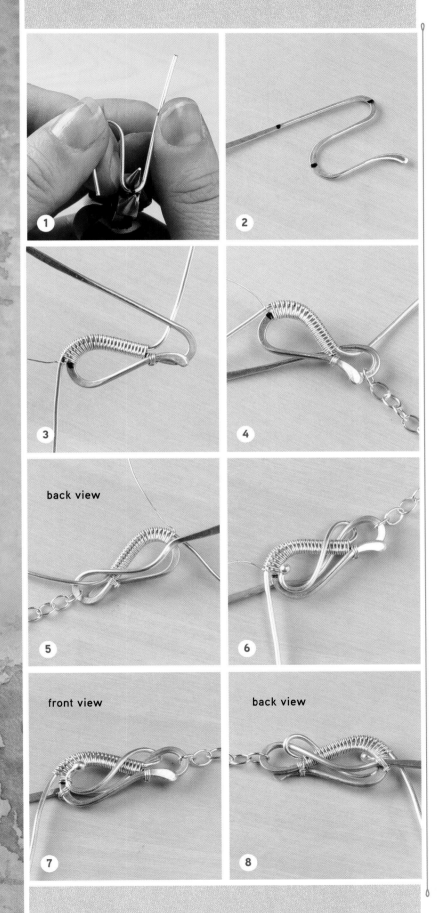

1

2

3

4

back view

5

6

front view

7

back view

8

forming the 18g wire

10 Flip the woven form over and bring the 18g wire (at the ⅝" [1.5 cm] mark) up and over the front of the weave, forming a loop. Bend the left side of the 18g wire so it follows the bottom inside of the larger curve. Using round-nose pliers, grasp the end of the 18g wire just below the ball, and curve the balled end inward **(Fig. 6)**.

11 Use the remaining 28g wire (the 6" [15 cm] tail wire) to lash the balled end of the 18g wire to the larger "U" of the 16g wire three times. Then lash the "U" and the 16g tail wire below it together (lashing just below the perpendicular section) three times. Thread your 28g wire through the lashing and wrap twice around the lashing to secure the 28g wire. Trim the excess wire **(Figs. 7 and 8)**.

12 Bend the remaining 18g wire so it curves around the large "U," over the lower section of the U-shaped curve, up across the shaped 18g wire and in front of the weave, ending up on the left side of the loop in the 18g wire.

13 Wrap the 18g wire around the back of the weave and under the paddled tail on the right, as shown. Using round-nose pliers, curve the balled end of the wire to the left as shown **(Fig. 9)**.

embellishing

14 Trim the perpendicular tail to ½" (1.3 cm). Grasp the tip of the tail with round-nose pliers and roll the wire up and over, "over-rolling" the wire onto itself, up to the 1" (2.5 cm) mark on the U-shaped wire **(Fig. 10)**. *tip: This loop needs to be large enough to slip onto the next link and should overlap itself in the back as shown.* **(Fig. 11)**

15 Using your fingers, bend the link over your thumb to give it a dome in front. You can also use the size 16 mark on the ring mandrel to shape the link using your fingers **(Fig. 12)**.

16 Cut a 4" (10 cm) length of 26g wire. String one pearl onto the center of the 26g wire. Wrap one end twice around the smaller balled end of the 18g wire that is lashed to the larger "U" of the 16g wire. Bring the other end across and under all three sections of the 18g wire on the right.

17 Lash the balled end of the 18g wire to the 18g wire below it twice. Secure both ends of the 26g wires by wrapping around the wire going through the pearl twice on either side of the pearl. Trim the excess 26g wire **(Fig. 13)**. *note: Steps 16–17 can be done with pre-oxidized 26g wire after you have oxidized and polished the bracelet in Step 22 if you are concerned about dipping your pearls in liver of sulfur.*

If you would like a bracelet larger than 7" (18 cm), add another link.

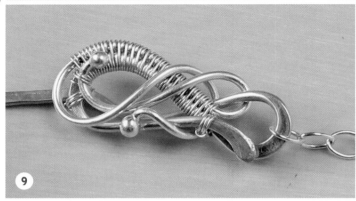

9

10

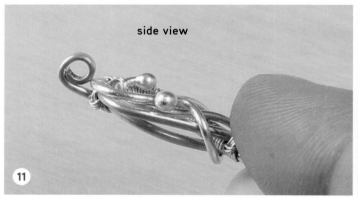

side view

11

12

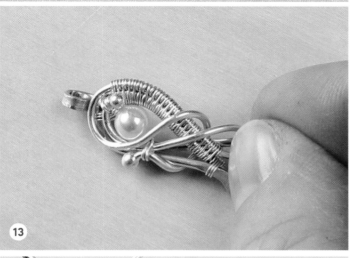

13

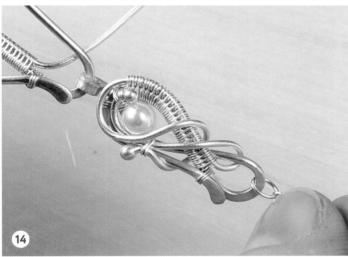

14

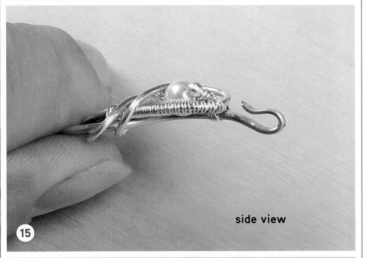

side view

15

creating the links

18 Make five more links by repeating Steps 3–17, except instead of adding the chain in Step 7, you will attach the loop on the end of the previous link as shown. **(Fig. 13)**. For the final link, instead of trimming the perpendicular tail, leave it the full length.

19 Round the end of the tail on the final link with the file and mark the center with the permanent marker. Bend the tail wire back from the lashings. Using round-nose pliers, bend the wire over at the center mark, forming a hook.

20 With the tip of the round-nose pliers, bend the end of the hook up slightly. Compress the hook so there is just enough clearance to slip on the chain **(Fig. 15)**.

It's very important that the finished length is as exact as possible when balling the wire. A ¹⁄₁₆" (2 mm) too long or short will affect the design. Remember that you don't need to ball up the wire all at once. Start with a small ball at the end of the wire and measure the length. If needed, melt the wire a little more and measure again. Continue until the wire is the right length.

finishing touches

21 Cut 3" (7.5 cm) of 24g wire and ball one end with the micro torch to create a head pin. String the remaining pearl onto the 24g wire and begin a wrapped loop. Slip the loop onto the last link on the chain and complete the wrap; trim the excess wire.

22 Oxidize the bracelet with liver of sulfur. Polish with the steel wool and brass brush. Use a polishing cloth or a tumbler to clean and brighten the jewelry.

variation

Make this copper version with burgundy pearls nestled inside the wire links and a pink crystal bicone dangle.

resources

Here is a list of my favorite places to shop.

Cherswee (Cheryl Sweeney)

cherswee.etsy.com

This is where I got my green bubble lampwork beads for the Ruffles and Lace Earrings variation (page 149).

Etsy

etsy.com

If I am looking for something unusual or can't find it locally, I love shopping Etsy's craft supply section.

Fusion Beads

fusionbeads.com

Fusion Beads has a wonderful selection of Swarovski crystals.

Monsterslayer

monsterslayer.com

This is my favorite place to buy fine silver wire.

Rings & Things

rings-things.com

Shop here for tools, pearls, and stones.

Rio Grande

riogrande.com

A great overall site to buy wire, findings, chains, and tools.

index

Love wire jewelry?

Check out other products and websites from Interweave!

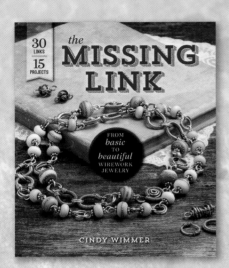

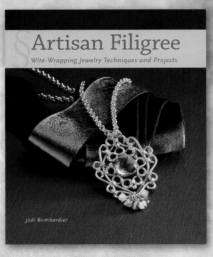

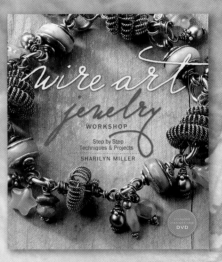

THE MISSING LINK
From Basic to Beautiful
Wirework Jewelry

Cindy Wimmer
ISBN: 9781596687073
Price: $22.95

ARTISAN FILIGREE
Wire-Wrapping Jewelry
Techniques and Projects

Jodi Bombardier
ISBN: 9781596686359
Price: $ 24.95

WIRE ART JEWELRY WORKSHOP
Step-by-Step Techniques
and Projects + DVD

Sharilyn Miller
ISBN: 9781596684089
Price: $ 26.95

JEWELRY MAKING DAILY

If you love jewelry, you'll feel at home at jewelrymakingdaily.com! Learn about Interweave's newest jewelry making books and magazines, access articles and projects in free ebooks, and treat your eyes to ,jewelry blogs, galleries, newsletters and more!

STEP BY STEP WIRE JEWELRY

Discover the newest in wire jewelry trends with *Step by Step Wire Jewelry* magazine!